Reforming Marlowe

Reforming Marlowe

The Nineteenth-Century Canonization
of a Renaissance Dramatist

Thomas Dabbs

Lewisburg
Bucknell University Press
London and Toronto: Associated University Presses

Associated University Presses
440 Forsgate Drive
Cranbury, NJ 08512

Associated University Presses
25 Sicilian Avenue
London WC1A 2QH, England

Associated University Presses
P.O. Box 39, Clarkson Pstl. Stn.
Mississauga, Ontario,
L5J 3X9 Canada

The paper used in this publication meets the requirements
of the American National Standard for Permanence of Paper
for Printed Library Materials Z39.48-984.

Library of Congress Cataloging-in-Publication Data

Dabbs, Thomas.
   Reforming Marlowe : the nineteenth-century canonization of a
Renaissance dramatist / Thomas Dabbs.
      p.   cm.
   Includes bibliographical references and index.
   ISBN 0-8387-5192-X
   1. Marlowe, Christopher, 1564–1593—Criticism and interpretation-
-History—19th century.   2. Criticism—Great Britain—History—19th
century.   3. Canon (Literature)   I. Title.
PR2674.D33   1991
822'.3—dc20   89-46399
                                                                               CIP

PRINTED IN THE UNITED STATES OF AMERICA

Contents

Acknowledgments

THIS project owes much to the encouragement and advice I received from my mentors and colleagues at the University of South Carolina. I would like to thank Professor Trevor Howard-Hill for his expert perspectives from the enormous and complex field of Renaissance bibliography. I also owe a special thanks to Professor Patrick Scott. Without the benefit of his knowledge of nineteenth-century publication and reception, this project would not have been possible. I would also like to thank Professor Meili Steele for his help in the field of critical theory. Finally, I would like to express my deepest and most sincere appreciation to Professor Arthur Kinney of the University of Massachusetts, Amherst, for his careful and learned commentary.

I am also indebted to a number of my peers who provided advice on various portions of this project. I owe much thanks to Barry Faulk, Andrew Shifflet, and Marc Demarest for a series of long and lively discussions in the areas of literary history and critical theory. I would also like to thank Betsy Baker, Sue Tully, Laurie Demarest, and Neil Johnson, for their general suggestions and assistance. Finally, I would like to express my gratitude to David Miller for his patient advice concerning chapter 2 of this study.

I would also like to express my appreciation to officers and members of the Marlowe Society and specifically to Professor Constance Kuriyama of Texas Tech University for her editorial guidance on what became the first chapter of this project. I am also deeply indebted to Professor Brian Striar of the University of North Florida for his sponsorship and support in the field of Marlowe studies.

Finally, I would like to extend my most grateful appreciation to family and friends for their continued love and support during the *annus mirabilis* during which this project was largely completed.

Life Sketch

THE reader who is not familiar with scholarship on Christopher Marlowe may benefit from a brief sketch of the information that scholars have compiled to date concerning the playwright's life and works.

Christopher Marlowe (1564–93) was born in Canterbury, the son of an established shoemaker. He attended King's School, Canterbury, and was awarded a scholarship to Corpus Christi, Cambridge, where he completed his B.A. in 1584. Most scholars agree that even though he continued at Cambridge he was covertly employed in some form of governmental service at this time. It was rumored that he expressed an interest in entering the English seminary in Rheims as a convert to Catholicism, a report which of course disturbed the university authorities at Cambridge. The Privy Council intervened on his behalf, however, and his M.A. was conferred in 1587.

The events of his short professional life have been the source of an enormous amount of scholarly debate and speculation concerning his character and the authorship of his plays. He was apparently the author of both parts of *Tamburlaine*. He also wrote *The Tragical History of Dr. Faustus*, *The Jew of Malta*, and *Edward II*. *Dido, Queen of Carthage* has been attributed either partly or completely to Marlowe, and a fragment entitled *The Massacre at Paris* has also been ascribed to him. He was also a poet and a translator in the Ovidian tradition. His *Hero and Leander,* an unfinished work that was completed by Chapman, is heralded as one of the finest examples of sixteenth-century narrative verse. His innovative verse style and his outrageous characters and themes have won him an enormous amount of critical attention in the field of Renaissance drama.

Nineteenth- and twentieth-century scholarship has uncovered fragmented but crucial evidence concerning the playwright's life and associations that indicates he was involved with certain subversive elements in and around London during his short life. Marlowe was arrested in May 1593 after he was charged with blasphemy on a document provided by the playwright Thomas Kyd. On 1 June 1593 he was stabbed to death by a man named Ingram Friser in a Deptford tavern and was buried nearby.

Reforming Marlowe

Introduction

Valdes: Faustus, these books, thy wit, and our experience
Shall make all nations to canonize us.

ALTHOUGH this book is tied specifically to the subject of Christopher Marlowe, it seeks to present ideas that expand far beyond the study of one sixteenth-century playwright. Chiefly, through examining how one significant literary figure was rediscovered and historicized during the nineteenth century, this project ultimately attempts to show the lasting influence of certain modes of critical thinking that came into being during the past century. The example of Marlowe's canonization is perfect for a study of this nature. As scholars have repeatedly pointed out, little was said or even known about Marlowe until the nineteenth century. Moreover, no literary historical figure rose to prominence more quickly or more forcefully than Marlowe during this period. This sudden appreciation afforded to Marlowe's life and works therefore reflects a distinctly nineteenth-century change in the way literary history was perceived by men of letters.

Marlowe's rise during this period also provides an in-depth and intriguing look at certain nineteenth-century ideologies at work. The damning accounts of Marlowe's life and the intemperate nature of the playwright's dramatic characters indicated to our predecessors that he was a violent rogue who was given to blasphemy and sexual excess. One wonders why such a character would suddenly be given such high esteem during a period that is typified by its religious austerity and rigid social standards. The way in which Marlowe was heralded in the past century, therefore, reflects the complexities and contradictions that surrounded the general effort to promote historical literature during that time.

With the general objective of learning more about the origins and influences of nineteenth-century thought, this study seeks specifically to analyze nineteenth-century views of Marlowe's life and work in order to trace these early interpretations from their specific social, economic, and political origins. Moreover, the sources of certain perceptions of Marlowe, whether they are founded on concrete evidence or mere rumor, will be analyzed in critical works and editions throughout the century. After doing so it should become clear that Marlowe was originally invented by Victorian scholars, critics, and educators and then handed on to us. Finally, this study also forwards the larger notion that our views of all literary history are still tainted by nineteenth-century biases.

In order to justify the critical importance that has been assigned to this project, however, a short defense must be made of the theoretical assumptions that justify this investigation. Regardless of certain poststructuralist (and, in fact, "New Critical") efforts to distance the consideration of the author from the text, this study is founded on the understanding that what is known or believed about the lives of various authors is a primary force in the presentation and interpretation of their works. Many of the observations made in the following pages, moreover, are supported by recent theoretical approaches that have sought to rejuvenate the consideration of certain ignored historical texts in order to challenge standard views of literary history.

Given the critical license to reevaluate our understanding of the literary past, this study attempts to disentangle Marlowe from some of the enduring myths that have surrounded him by examining the history of his critical reception. This, however, is not a typical reception study. Traditionally, studies of this nature gather the observations of certain critics on a significant literary figure either to create a coterie from their written opinions or, as in the case of Tucker Brooke's study of Marlowe's reputation, to provide a bibliographical map of all the noteworthy responses to an otherwise stable author.[1] While it is a valuable contribution to scholarship, Brooke's study does not attempt to view Marlowe as a shifting signifier that was transformed by the economic, social, and political setting of each significant critical event. Moreover, Brooke does not suggest that like their nineteenth-century predecessors twentieth-century editors, researchers, and critics may also be slow to abandon certain notions of Marlowe's life and work that were founded on fabrications and conjectures.

It is not enough, however, simply to demonstrate that the interpretation of Marlowe's life and work was shaped by later schools of thought. It is common knowledge, for example, that romanticism inspired a unique understanding of Shakespeare and other Renaissance playwrights. This discussion, therefore, not only examines how Marlowe was positioned within certain cultural movements of the nineteenth century, but it also attempts to determine the precise historical location of these movements. For instance, there was certainly a "romantic" Marlowe, but this view of the playwright did not surface until the 1870s, when Victorian educators began to establish a "romantic" canon of early nineteenth-century poets. Moreover, this study argues that certain Victorian arrangements of literary history still influence our own readings of Marlowe. In short, although our research methods are far more precise than those of the prior century, the way in which we interpret our data is still deeply rooted in Victorian critical polemics. This endeavor, therefore, concentrates on exposing, and thus undermining, the bibliographical "history" of Marlowe chiefly by examining the ideologies that colored the presentation of his life and works.

In order to clarify the specific critical approach of this study, it is necessary to present a basic concept that has been fundamental to recent readings of literary history. In a now famous essay entitled "What Is an Author," Michel Foucault admits that certain texts have an "author function" that attributes itself to textual interpretation. He states that an author's name "does not pass from the interior of a discourse to the real and exterior individual who produced it; instead, the name seems always to be present, marking off the edges of the text, revealing, or at least characterizing, its mode of being."[2] Foucault's point here becomes even more important when one examines the entire history of an author's reception by another culture. In this case, one must examine not only how the author's name "marks off the edge" of the text; one must also consider how it provides an additional cohesive edge to another set of texts that have been placed within a general description of the author's era. Without reception and critical reproduction there may be no discourse on the matter of authorial presence at all because the author's text may be lost in some dark archive. In short, the way in which authors are perceived is crucial to the production and critical assessment of their texts. Moreover, the way in which these texts are privileged, presented, and distributed is intricately tied to certain theoretical notions of how they should be read.

The most noteworthy theoretical explanation of the overall method that has been utilized in this study is provided by Edward Said in his *Orientalism*. While discussing the way in which certain authoritative notions of the Orient have been produced by Western culture, Said says that Orientalism "is directly indebted to various Western techniques of representation that make the Orient visible, clear, 'there' in discourse about it." However, Said notes also that these representations "rely upon institutions, traditions, conventions, agreed-upon codes of understanding for their effects, not upon a distant and amorphous Orient."[3]

Just as the "West" established its own definitive discourse on the "Oriental other," the nineteenth-century man of letters established a set of discursive formulas around the works of sixteenth- and early seventeenth-century English authors. This study examines the discursive formation of Marlowe in the nineteenth century and, to an extent, the formation of the "other era" in which he lived. Although no events of the sixteenth or seventeenth centuries are discussed here in any great detail, the Renaissance is still the general subject of this discussion, which seeks to expose, in a small way, the "Renaissance" that was assembled and bequeathed to us by the Victorian academy and by other nineteenth-century literary institutions. In fact, the notion of sixteenth-century English literature signaling a renaissance itself is essentially the creation of nineteenth-century criticism. Although we think of our interpretive methodologies as being far removed from those of the past century, most students who take a course in Shakespeare or Renaissance drama are still exposed to literary theories that are indebted to middle-class Victorian notions of social (or "natural") order and unity.

This project, therefore, provides primarily a genealogy of the cultural foundation upon which a "Marlowe" was constructed. Specifically, the establishment of Marlowe's biography came about through a complex set of critical efforts that sought to provide an acceptable persona for the handful of sixteenth-century plays and poems ascribed to the playwright. The study of turns this persona takes in the nineteenth century provides fertile ground for speculations deeply rooted in cultural hermeneutics and particularly in the social and political biases of Victorian reception.

The question remains as to what can be gained by a study of this nature. First of all, nowhere among sixteenth-century writers has the "author function" been so traceable as in the case of Marlowe. His abrupt revival in the nineteenth century tells us much about the underlying critical machinery that reproduced historical texts during that period. Although one may be inclined to think that nineteenth-century interpretations of Marlowe may merely be stepped over by reading a textual edition of the playwright's works and drawing one's own conclusions, the printing of the edition itself was mandated by nineteenth-century critical precedents. Far more readers in our century have read an individual play by Marlowe than by Brome or, for that matter, even Ford or Chapman. *Faustus,* for instance, is almost mandatory for undergraduate English majors. At the beginning of the nineteenth century, however, Ford, Chapman, and even Brome were generally considered to be more important than Marlowe. Moreover, the general status of Renaissance drama was far lower than it is today. In fact there would be no impetus for reading Marlowe, nor would there be any readily accessible editions of his work, were it not for the critical evaluations of Victorian men of letters.

The idea that one can draw "individual" conclusions from Renaissance texts is one of the enduring myths of New Critical thought. Any edition of Marlowe's works is intricately tied to a long history of textual interpretations—interpretations that have influenced the dating of his plays, the arrangement of acts and scenes, and even the placement of individual words on the printed page. Most of these textual decisions are deeply embedded in the specific social and political structures of past cultures.

This study, however, does not focus on the textual history of Marlowe's plays but considers how a perceived "Marlowe" affects the presentation of the works ascribed to him. The interpretations and manipulations of Marlowe's biography are examined in order to demonstrate how Victorian researchers, educators, and critics placed the playwright within various canons of study. The exposure of the social, political, and personal motives of various Victorian researchers and critics is important to our understanding of Marlowe, therefore, not so that we can have additional information, but so that we may be able to distinguish the bibliographical facts concerning Marlowe's life and works from the interpretive fictions that have affected their presentation.

This study also provides a serendipitous journey through less clearly charted regions of nineteenth-century letters. A distinct feature of Marlowe's nineteenth-century reception is that most of the major poets of the period had little to say about him. Wordsworth, Coleridge, Arnold, Tennyson, and other prestigious poetical figures virtually avoided Marlowe, while certain "less important" critics such as Lamb, Hazlitt, Hunt, Dowden, Swinburne, and others openly supported the playwright. Although this may be a historical accident, it suggests that much of the literary innovation for which the nineteenth century is famous came about through the work of lesser-known critics. Probing deeper, one finds that Marlowe's writings were also supported behind the scenes by seldom studied but influential publishers, editors, and researchers. An examination of Marlowe's reception during this period, therefore, provides a reason to look into the efforts of William Pickering, J.P. Collier, Alexander Dyce, and many others who collectively provided the impetus for what, in the later portion of the century, became an organized movement to reproduce old texts. In fact, the attention paid to Marlowe by those who were chiefly men of letters rather than poets doubtlessly marks the beginning of a separate and distinct critical industry.

By following a revised understanding of the nineteenth century, this study holds that the "romantic" period was, like the "Renaissance," a historical classification of literature that was established by Victorian men of letters. Therefore, the Victorian sense of literary history will be examined in terms of how histories during this period were constructed under the auspices of then current philosophical paradigms. As will be seen, these distinctions are of great importance to the understanding of Marlowe's growing prestige throughout the century.

Chapter 1 begins during the eighteenth century in order to demonstrate that Marlowe was a virtually unknown literary figure during that time. Among eighteenth-century critics in general, old plays were considered to have limited literary value. The exception to this rule was Robert Dodsley's edition of *Old Plays* (1744), which was a painstaking effort to provide a selection of little-known English plays from hundreds of ignored quartos. Although Marlowe's *Edward II* appears in this edition, his is only one among many plays placed in the series. By the end of the century, however, Marlowe had become more prominent in the estimation of scholars, critics, and collectors, but his reputation as a depraved atheist may have put off critical consideration of his works. Although it seems that he was read and studied privately, he was, for the most part, avoided publicly until the turn of the nineteenth century.

The early 1800s, however, saw the advent of a new form of critical inquiry and a growing market for old plays. Beginning with the excerpted passages of Renaissance drama in Charles Lamb's *Specimens,* dramatic poetry was considered in terms of an overarching artistic theory that gave more credence to the qualities of vigor and sensation than it did to the standards of decorum and convention. Marlowe's work was given a generous amount of space by Lamb, and later by Hazlitt, who ventured to praise Marlowe's work openly. Paralleling this critical phenomenon, Marlowe's plays were included in a growing number of series that were, in essence, remakes of Dodsley. Finally, an 1818 production of *The Jew of Malta* brought a Marlovian drama to the London stage for the first time in over a century and a half.

It seems that the new market for Marlowe's plays inspired the Pickering edition of Marlowe's *Works.* Essentially, by the end of the Regency, Marlowe's works had gained status because adventurous critics had commented on his works and because his plays enjoyed some popularity in a growing market for old drama.

Ultimately, because Marlowe enjoyed more market value, critics began to defend him against accusations that had been made against him by earlier biographers. The foundation of serious Marlowe scholarship, therefore, is the subject of chapter 2. The work of James Broughton, J. P. Collier, and Alexander Dyce, which took place in the second quarter of the nineteenth century, is examined closely in order to determine why misconceptions concerning Marlowe's life continued to run rampant. Although these three researchers made pioneering discoveries about Marlowe's life and works, they misrepresented the playwright in certain places for a variety of reasons. Collier is primarly at fault for many enduring misconceptions about Marlowe because he intentionally forged and manipulated key historical documents. Although early Marlowe research was amazingly accurate, it left a legacy of doubt chiefly concerning Marlowe's biography.

Because of certain features of the playwright's life and work, he was swept into an essentially Victorian debate in which matters of the past were polemically charged to argue present concerns. For instance, it has been noted by critics that the era that is known for moral restraint and industry also valued the idealism and even the excesses given to romantic thought. As mentioned above, Victorian critics were in fact responsible for inventing the *post facto* concept of the romantic "period" long after the Regency had ended. Marilyn Butler points out that the term *romantic* is "anachronistic" and that the "poets concerned would not have used it of themselves." She further notes that "not until the 1860s did 'the Romantics' become an accepted collective name for Blake, Wordsworth, Coleridge, Scott, Byron, Shelley, and Keats, and an agreement begin to emerge about what an English Romantic Poet was like."[4] Indeed, this discussion will avoid grouping the literary critics of the early nineteenth century in terms of a general romantic sensibility.

This apparent paradox in the Victorian cultural consciousness pulled the interpretation of Marlowe in two contradictory directions. Some critics tried to make Marlowe out to be an artistic moral reformist, while others lauded what they perceived as his romantic contempt for authority. There were also a few who attempted to reconcile these conflicting views of the playwright by arguing that he was essentially a moral idealist who was corrupted by the hypocrisy of his times. All Victorian evaluations of Marlowe, however, share the common tendency to project certain private and public concerns onto the playwright's life and works.

The second half of the nineteenth century saw the advent of English studies and the establishment of a generally romantic literary theory that was employed to a degree by both conservative educators and the literary avant-garde. Moreover, in part because of the bibliographical discoveries of early-century scholars and in part because of the prestige that early-century poets had invested in Renaissance poetic forms, later Victorians began to give Renaissance literature more regard than ever before. In this environment Marlowe became an attractive subject for critics from roughly the mid-century onward because he was part of what had come to be seen as a great movement in English letters.

Marlowe also gained a much higher status in comparison with his Renaissance contemporaries. This dramatic change in the playwright's reception came about for two reasons: first, Collier had established that Marlowe had a direct influence on Shakespeare, and second, the playwright's manipulated and forged biography was likened to the lives of Shelley, Byron, and others who themselves were

gaining prestige under the growing influence of Continental romanticism. Ironically, the features of Marlowe's life that had apparently
made him an anathema to the neoclassicals made him one of the most
praiseworthy examples of the Renaissance sensibility to many Victorians. By the end of the nineteenth century, Marlowe was in fact
seen by many to be second only to Shakespeare as a Renaissance
dramatist.

Marlowe's higher standing was also the result of random conjectures
and baseless assumptions. Often critics even made up their own
scenarios for Marlowe's life on no authority at all. Essentially, though,
there clearly became two Marlowes in the second half of the nineteenth century: one established by Victorian educators and the other
dreamed up by the late-century literari. Both images of Marlowe were
based on hearsay, forgery, and conjecture, and to an extent both have
endured throughout the twentieth century.

The way in which Marlowe was affected by the effort to provide
English education for the middle classes is the subject of chapter 3.
Beginning with the Society for the Advancement of Useful Knowledge and the birth of the "educational" literary history, Marlowe
entries become more and more random depending on the historical
angle of each individual author. By the 1860s, when "textbook"
histories began to appear, Marlowe was usually made out to be a
moral reformist. By the 1870s, however, with the help of a type of
transcendental romanticism that was applied to Renaissance literature
by Edward Dowden, Marlowe began to be viewed as a passionate
idealist. His excesses were seen an essential feature of his moral
character because they were interpreted as the result of his frustrated
effort to achieve perfection in art. This view of Marlowe won the
Victorian academy and, through the criticism of A. C. Bradley and
others, still survives in some quarters to this day.

On the "other" side, Marlowe was adopted by the late-century
literati who provided wild and extravagant images of the playwright in
order to maintain an ongoing resistance against Victorian political and
social values. These figures are the focus of chapter 4. Beginning in
1837 with R. H. Horne's "The Death of Christopher Marlowe," the
radical camp portrayed Marlowe as a passionate and rebellious romantic. Leigh Hunt also supplemented this image in *Imagination and
Fancy*. Although this view of Marlowe as a radical never took hold in
the literary community, the reprinting of Horne's play in an 1885

edition of Marlowe's *Works* fueled highly abstract and flamboyant views of the playwright that were provided by A. C. Swinburne, J. A. Symonds, and to some extent Havelock Ellis. These conflicting interpretations of Marlowe in the nineteenth century have been at the source of many critical controversies over the playwright during the twentieth. Many recent conclusions reached about Marlowe's political, moral, and sexual affinities are rooted in speculations provided by the late nineteenth-century literati.

This study does not pretend to provide a thorough bibliographical survey of Marlowe in the nineteenth century, although it does cover the major trends and vogues into which the playwright was incorporated. Also, certain areas have been examined more closely than others because they were considered especially influential on later thought. Marlowe, for instance, was a novelty at the beginning of the century. By the end, however, he was a widely known and notorious literary figure. A small statement made about Marlowe in 1820 is far more important, therefore, than a statement of similar proportions made in 1890. Also, Broughton, Collier, and Dyce are examined more closely than later Marlowe scholars because their bibliographical discoveries provided the foundation for Marlowe studies.

Several general categories have been provided in order to clarify the nature of the intellectual forces that influenced studies on Marlowe during this period. The distinction between the literary surveys of academe and the criticism of the literati is enlightening but somewhat flawed. Most critics, whether educators or professional men of letters, read the same journals and were influenced by the same intellectual trends. Some, like Dowden, were both professional critics and educators. However, the distinction serves to illuminate the fundamental concerns of each group and is therefore helpful. Furthermore, while some assumptions have been made about attitudes or events that cannot be clearly documented, this discussion for the most part only considers textual evidence that appears either in manuscript or in print. For the most part, we are only able to make inferences about Marlowe's reception from what "they" allowed us to see.

Although this study is not purely theoretical, several literary philosophers have been present in spirit. Foucault's method of writing disruptive histories of institutions provided the scholarly impetus for assembling this "history" of Renaissance reception. A more specific methodological influence, however, has been Said's perspective on how various interrelated discourses establish an authoritative field of interpretation that is divorced from the "actual" area of concern. Finally, Paul Bove, who has lately become the "Darth Vader" of institutional criticism, contributed to the spirit of this project as it is ultimately a statement on how the radical is inducted and consumed by the institution.

Closer at hand has been the work of a number of scholars whose research has been fundamental to this study. Richard Altick and John Gross have provided much of the bibliographical foundation on which this discussion stands by presenting clear, useful, and abundant data on nineteenth-century publication and readership. Marilyn Butler, Jerome McGann, Chris Baldick, Gerald Graff, and Terry Eagleton were also enormously helpful on the histories of certain literary and institutional trends during the nineteenth century. Many of the numerous biographers who have been consulted, from Sidney Lee to Phyllis Grosskurth, have provided useful and, indeed, crucial information. Finally, the extraordinary scholarship of Tucker Brooke, Frederick Boas, John Bakeless, Leslie Hotson, and others has supplied a wealth of information on Marlowe's biography and the publishing history of his works. All in all, this is a collective effort that draws together the research of many diverse and influential thinkers. I hope that the reader will find this examination of Marlowe's history not only professionally useful but also intellectually engaging.

1

The Discovery of Marlowe in the Early Nineteenth Century

OUR study of Christopher Marlowe owes more to the way he and his works were reassembled in the nineteenth century than perhaps we would like to admit. Were it not for the advent of a critical appreciation for old drama over 150 years after Marlowe's recorded death, we would have perhaps never heard of many Renaissance playwrights aside from Beaumont and Fletcher, Jonson, and Shakespeare. By the beginning of the eighteenth century most of the old play manuscripts and quartos that had survived the Elizabethan and Jacobean eras were thoroughly dispersed among random private collectors and book-sellers. While there was a conditional appreciation for the above-mentioned "major" playwrights, the general feeling among the neo-classicals was that most of the English plays written before the civil war were the unrefined expressions of a brutal and libertine sensibility.

Although Marlowe's life and work were taken into account in certain short biographies in the seventeenth and eighteenth centuries, the playwright was for the most part one of many names in a long list of English playwrights until the 1820s, when Hazlitt adventurously spoke of him as one who "stands high, and almost first" in a list of Shakespeare's contemporaries.[1] Before this, it is difficult to find such a high opinion of the dramatist or his work. *Tamburlaine, Faustus*, and *The Jew of Malta* were stage successes in their time; however, Marlowe's plays were not reprinted as often as the works of many of his contemporaries. Although it would be extremely difficult to rank him among dramatists during his own time, it is certain that many other Elizabethan and Jacobean playwrights and poets enjoyed more public and critical acclaim than did Marlowe. Shortly after Marlowe's plays were presented to the London stage, they fell into obscurity. Tucker

Brooke points out that the playwright's popularity had "shrunk to very small proportions" even before the end of the reign of James I; and afterwards, it soon "fell into almost total eclipse."[2]

Marlowe's work reappears in the mid-eighteenth century, however, when a fairly comprehensive list of old English dramatists was put together by Robert Dodsley for a select group of literary connoisseurs and antiquarians. Very little is known about Dodsley's early life, but it is certain that he rose from rustic and humble beginnings to become a respectable playwright and publisher. His series of old plays may be perhaps the single most important event in the critical rediscovery of Renaissance drama. The series certainly increased his own credibility in the eyes of his literary contemporaries. As Straus notes, "if there had been any question of his abilities before, all doubts must . . . have been dispelled, and his *Old Plays*, by which, indeed, he is best remembered at the present day, may be said to have been a permanent and important contribution to English literature."[3] As if often the case, the status of the works that were edited rose with the editor's own respectability.

The edition was begun after Dodsley, having succeeded commercially as a playwright and bookseller, purchased some seven hundred early editions of plays from Thomas Osborne of Gray's Inn. With the plays and with access to the theatrical library of his sponsor, Clement Cottrell Dormer, Dodsley was able to put together the first extensive and comprehensive collection of old plays in English history. After obtaining two hundred subscriptions, he also began a highly successful financial enterprise.[4] This undertaking provided not only the first canon of old English playwrights other than Beaumont and Fletcher, Jonson, and Shakespeare, but the first attempt to furnish a history of English drama. Dodsley's inclusion of *Edward II* also made a printed edition of Marlowe's then obscure work readily accessible to a select group of readers.

In his preface to the twelve-volume work (which is dedicated to Dormer), Dodsley evaluates English drama first by historicizing it and second by establishing the superiority of English dramatic efforts over the dramatic legacies of the French, the Germans, the Spanish, the Italians, and the Dutch. Dodsley defends the English dramatic tradition by correcting the misconception that the English stage evolved after other European cultures. He does this by quoting an "honest monk" of the fourteenth century named William Stephanides, or

Fitz-Stephen, who recorded that "interludes" in London were of a "more holy subject." Because Stephanides did not "mention these representations as novelties," Dodsley holds that the plays are much older than they were at the time of Stephanides' observation. Through this type of historical reasoning, Dodsley attempts to establish not only that English drama is "older" than European drama, but that it also has more sacred roots than the drama of other countries.[5]

In Dodsley's 1744 collection of English drama, one can see the numerous details that the editor had to manage in order to reconstruct a history of drama from random quartos and fragmented historical evidence. Dodsley's textual editing is meticulous and accurate. Before each of the many plays, he states what was known, if anything, about even the most minor figures. Especially when one considers that Dodsley was not a professional editor by our standards, the series was a mammoth accomplishment, and it greatly influenced editors of old drama for nearly 150 years after its appearance.

Dodsley's collection in fact fundamentally changed the way in which old English drama was to be interpreted. First of all, it provided a rough historical arrangement of the plays. Dodsley presented the old drama, which had previously been merely a random set of scattered and unedited stage spectacles, in a chronological pattern in order to demonstrate how it advanced from the medieval to the Shakesperean period. This presentation evidently made certain "unrefined" elements of the drama more acceptable to a learned class of literary connoisseurs because readers were encouraged to see the plays as early examples of a great dramatic tradition in the making.

Second, the fact that the plays were printed to be read (as opposed to being seen) by a fairly exclusive group of subscribers changed the original function of most and perhaps even all of the plays. We know with some certainty that most of these dramas, whether they were secular or religious, were originally popular events performed for a cross-section of society. Yet, from the "list of subscribers" after the preface of Dodsley's first edition, one can see from the titles that precede the names of many of the sponsors that the plays in Dodsley's series were not reproduced for popular consumption. Instead, they were accurately edited for a small group of affluent individuals, who, judging from Dodsley's preface, were to see these plays as valuable literary artifacts.

Although Dodsley elevated the appreciation for early English drama, he brought little notice to Marlowe. A close look at the overall series indicates that Marlowe remained a very minor figure by Dodsley's estimation. The playwright is not mentioned in the preface among his contemporaries Lyly, Heywood, and Lodge. Dodsley even quotes Heywood's prologue to *The Jew of Malta* without mentioning the name of the play's author.[6] In the dozens of plays printed in this twelve-volume series, Marlowe's work is given no more notice than *Damon and Pithias* by Richard Edwards and *The Shepherd's Holiday* by Joseph Rutter. Yet, although the edition treats Marlowe no differently than these minor playwrights, it does preserve *Edward II* for the scrutiny of future critics.

Marlowe's Reputation during the Eighteenth Century

During the years after the first edition of Dodsley, there is little evidence that Marlowe's status rose above his barely noticable placement in the *Old Plays*. Aside from commenting on certain major dramatic figures, men of letters seemed content to let small individual dramatists like Marlowe remain obscure. Toward the end of the century, however, several things happened that indicate that Marlowe received some notable private consideration among the literati.

In the second edition of Dodsley's *Old Plays* (1780), the new editor, Isaac Reed, adds *The Jew of Malta*, giving Marlowe two plays and thus making the playwright a more considerable presence within the Dodsley format. Although this indicates Reed's greater appreciation for Marlowe, the editor omits the playwright's name from his discussion of the "early efforts" of English playwrights and the ephemeral nature of dramatic characters and their creators.

> Congreve, Vanbrugh, and Cibber now exhibit characters almost as obsolete as those of Ben Jonson, or Beaumont and Fletcher; and if such names as the latter cannot ensure a continuance of fame, the Dekkars, Middletons, Chapmans, and Marstons, their contemporaries, must give up their claim to immortality without a murmur.[7]

Now that Marlowe has two plays included in the series, his absence from Reed's list of whom he sees as only minor Elizabethan playwrights (Decker et al.) is conspicuous.

Regardless of his apparent appreciation for Marlowe, Reed may have been hesitant to praise the playwright openly in a literary society that sought to sustain lofty notions of taste and refinement. Reed had more than enough reason to slight Marlowe in this fashion, if that is what he was doing. For instance, as in the first edition, he prefaces each play with a biography of its writer. The biography provided for Marlowe by Dodsley and then repeated by Reed comprises first a 1597 indictment by Thomas Beard in *The Theatre of God's Judgement*. This account exposes a playwright named Marlowe as an impious atheist and a social degenerate.[8] It is the first among a series of biographical speculations that are later repeated by Anthony à Wood, in 1691, almost one hundred years after Marlowe's reported death. The Beard account, along with a short reference by Francis Meres, is embellished by Wood to indicate that this Marlowe was overcome and killed by a servant in a fight over another serving woman.[9] These stories of Marlowe's base affiliations, along with the reports of his atheism, would of course make him an anathema to the readers of Reed's second edition (see Appendix A).[10]

Whatever growing appreciation there may have been for Marlowe during the late eighteenth century, therefore, was either expressed with caution or not expressed at all. In his *History of English Poetry* (1774), Thomas Warton, an Oxford Poetry professor and Spenserian, ventures to give Marlowe credit for being "one of the most distinguished tragic poets of his age."[11] Yet later, after damning *Faustus* as a silly play, he allows Marlowe literary rank only by virtue of his poetry.[12] Warton's liberalism was harshly challenged, however, in 1782, when Joseph Ritson, the acerbic critic who censured the Steevens edition of Shakespeare and also Reed's textual criticism, condemned Warton for saying anything positive about Marlowe.

> I have great respect for Marlow as an ingenious poet, but I have a much higher regard for truth and justice; and will therefore take the liberty to produce the strongest (if not the whole) proof that now remains of his [Marlowe's] diabolical tenets, and debauched morals.[13]

After this reprimand, Ritson published Baines's famous indictment of Marlowe's character, which contends that Marlowe made a series of outlandishly blasphemous remarks (see Appendix B).[14] The publication of this note was the most condemning and damaging assessment of Marlowe's character that ever had been presented to a reading public.

Ritson's short, self-righteous jab at Warton is telling because as a critic he is arguing that the value of Marlowe's works could not be considered apart from the morality of the playwright himself. Moreover, Ritson clearly states that no matter what artistic accomplishments Marlowe may have achieved, his works should not be held highly because he was reported to be an immoral man. This type of thinking eventually became the target of many critics in the nineteenth century who became defenders of Marlowe's drama and poetry.[15] For many years, however, these charges of debauchery, criminal behavior, and, of course, atheism seemingly restricted the public acclaim of anything having to do with Marlowe.

A covert interest in Marlowe and his assumed works did begin to emerge in the latter part of the eighteenth century within certain literary clubs or circles. Because of the constant exchange of ideas and information that flowed among the members of these groups, they were of central importance to literary scholars such as Reed, Edmond Malone, and even to some extent George Steevens and David Garrick, all of whose efforts affected the way in which the old English plays were circulated and interpreted. It seems, too, as if these and other literary collectors privately admired Marlowe's writings. Brooke notes that scholars and actors began to seek out rare Marlovian quartos. Some, notably Isaac Reed, were especially interested in obtaining editions of Marlowe. Malone even managed to assemble a private collection of Marlowe's complete works by binding together early editions of his plays. Garrick, too, collected quartos of Marlowe's plays for his private library.[16]

While one should not be overly anxious to reach large conclusions with so little evidence, something should be said about the absence of Marlowe in some literary arenas of the late eighteenth century that was made conspicuous by his presence in others. Certain men of letters had an antiquarian interest in Marlowe's plays, yet, at least in the cases of Malone, Reed, and Garrick, they avoided evaluating Marlowe's work in a public forum, either by critically reassessing him or, in Garrick's case, by presenting his drama to members of a playgoing society.

Unlike most of Marlowe's companions in the Dodsley series, some speculative but highly engaging evidence of his atheism and degeneracy survived more as a result of historical mischance than anything else. Yet this evidence, it seems, inhibited open critical discussions of Marlowe's work. Although the playwright's reputation repelled the polite and conservative man of letters, it seems, the quality of his dramatic poetry enticed the literary scholar. One is limited, though, in how to interpret these brief traces of Marlowe during the late eighteenth century because so little information is on record. It is certain that Marlowe's reputation as a scoundrel who died in a tavern cursing God and the Trinity was well-known among the literati, and his life-style, it seems, was far too socially unacceptable for his works to gain public approval from most established scholars or critics. It was not until the nineteenth century, when Marlowe's works would be decontextualized and assessed by a critical method that permitted authorial excess, that the critical establishment provided him any rank.

The Turn of the Nineteenth Century

Regardless of the cautious attention that Marlowe received in the late eighteenth century, the playwright was generally considered by critics during this period as only a minor dramatist who had little historical importance. In the first half of the nineteenth century, however, Marlowe came to be regarded as one of the finer examples of Renaissance dramaturgy. Marlowe's complete works would see certainly three editions by 1850. Also, in the 1810s and 1820s the dramatic "series," which are covered below, began including both *Faustus* and *Dido* (see both C. W. Dilke collections and *Old English Drama*, respectively). "Hero and Leander" also went through three editions. The poem was included in Sir Egerton Brydges's *Restituta* (1815), in Chapple's *Old English Poets* (1820), and in Singer's *Select English Poets* (1821). *The Jew of Malta* and *Faustus* were also altered and edited in several separate editions, the most important of which were the Penley and Oxberry editions covered below. By mid-century, Marlowe began to enjoy a position "next to Shakespeare," which was comparable with that of Jonson and Beaumont and Fletcher.

Marlowe's sudden popularity in the nineteenth century requires a detailed analysis, for he is the only Elizabethan or Jacobean playwright whose status changed so greatly in such a short period of time.

A major problem for Marlowe scholars during this period, for instance, was rooted in how to approach an author whose reported depravity made it unseemly for a critic to approve of his works. Furthermore, just how was one to praise Marlowe's achievements in plays such as *The Jew of Malta* and *Edward II*, in which anti-Semitism and homosexuality are dramatized in such a forthright and outlandish manner? Essentially, Marlowe could not emerge as a major figure until a form of critical inquiry was developed that allowed an appreciation for Marlowe's verse without calling too much attention either to his life or to the overall themes of his works.

The Specimens of Charles Lamb

The reconstruction of the British dramatic canon continued in the nineteenth century, but the nature of scholarship directed toward the old dramatic poets was changed with the introduction, in 1808, of the *Specimens of English Dramatic Poets*, selected by Charles Lamb.[17] This work is an important event in the study of old drama, not so much because of Lamb's brief glosses of the excerpts he presents, but because of the anatomy of the critical package itself. Essentially, Lamb's perception of Marlowe and other old dramatists made certain obscure plays available for public consumption and attractive to the literary novice. He also arranged and glossed the dramatic material in a way that lent artistic credence to dramas that many prior critics had found unrefined.

The "specimens" are poetic excerpts from over seventy old playwrights, many of whom had been represented in Dodsley's series. Lamb, however, notes that over one-third of the plays he considers could be found only in the British Museum. The first unique feature of this work, therefore, is that it can be read almost as if it were a museum catalogue that functions to expose the reader to little-known treasures from literary antiquity. It presents not entire plays but brief selections of speeches taken out of context for their poetical merit and for other interesting or remarkable features.

By stringing together excerpts from the original drama, Lamb in fact constructs another textual body that, although delivered with little commentary, is heavily influenced by his own critical judgment.

To every extract is prefixed an explanatory head, sufficient to make it intelligible with the help of some trifling omissions. Where a line or more was obscure, as having reference to something that had gone before, which would have asked more time to explain than its consequence in the scene seemed to deserve, I have had no hesitation in leaving the line or passage out. Sometimes where I have met with a superfluous character, which seemed to burthen without throwing any light upon the scene, I have ventured to dismiss it altogether.[18]

By an "explanatory head," Lamb of course means a short heading that ostensibly provides information to make the passage more understandable. Yet, what Lamb in fact does provide is a "head" or thinking organ to an otherwise lifeless body of textual excerpts that directs the reader toward a particular interpretation. In terms of their literary function, these excerpts provide an entirely new text, one that serves to provide the distinct features of a perceived literary era.

The Marlowe section is characteristic of Lamb's treatment of the other dramatists, although Lamb gives Marlowe's work a generous amount of space during a time when little was known about the playwright. It is not difficult to see how the works then attributed to Marlowe provided many attractive specimens to an editor whose purpose seems far less evaluative than expository. In the context of this work, Marlowe's plays have an extraordinary appeal. Lamb begins the section with a scene in which the Queen Mother of Spain solicits the love of Eleazar, the Moor, in *Lusts Dominion, or the Lascivious Queen*, a play that was then ascribed to Marlowe. This image of the wanton Queen proposing to the reluctant Moor that "In my all-naked arms thyself shalt lie" is followed by an excerpt from Tamburlaine that vividly describes the muscular frame of the Scythian conqueror. The dynamic physical description of Tamburlaine is followed by perhaps the most provoking speech of Gaveston in *Edward II*, during which he describes how he plans to delight his lover the king. This speech is followed by a variety of other scenes that, were we unfamiliar with the playwright, would certainly arouse our interest in him even further. For instance, the reader is given a glimpse of Edward's encounter with Lightborn before his assassination and Faustus's disquieted plea for God's mercy before his tragic demise.[19]

While tantalizing his readers with a glimpse of the sensations of Marlovian drama, Lamb also seeks to lend prestige to the ignored work of Marlowe and other Elizabethan and Jacobean dramatists by using several arguments for their artistic importance. Chiefly, he stresses the "Shakespearean" characteristics of their works. Lamb in fact argues that these passages are valuable specifically because they reveal "how much of Shakspeare shines in the great men his contemporaries."[20] Here Lamb is suggesting, too, that a dramatic speech in a poet's play reveals certain qualities "in" the dramatic poet. It is further assumed that the personal qualities of Shakespeare can be recognized in the poetry of other dramatists. Although this may be true, Lamb never specifically states exactly what poetic (and indeed personal) features Marlowe and other lesser known dramatists share with Shakespeare.

The obvious ambiguity of Lamb's statement is not a critical flaw, but an essential component of a methodology that is used to make a little-known body of literature more attractive to his audience. By hand-picking certain exciting dramatic moments and presenting them for perusal, Lamb piques the reader's interest in obscure and, in many cases, unpublished plays in much the same way that a clip from a forthcoming film engages the interest of a potential viewer. Also, by affiliating these writers thematically and personally with an accepted and revered author such as Shakespeare, Lamb provides them much more prestige than they were generally given during his time.

While the late eighteenth-century man of letters may have been reluctant to praise Marlowe because of the air of irreverence that surrounded his life and works, Lamb seems more than willing to present scenes that seemingly scandalize the playwright even more than before. Lamb was, no doubt, drawn to the reports of Marlowe's unorthodox life, and he obviously was trying to publicize this unorthodoxy in the dramatic samples that he chose (although one does not have to look long or hard to find potentially irreverent material in Marlowe's works). During a time in which poets and critics were distancing themselves from neoclassical standards and manners, examples of excessive behavior in the lives of poets had become not only acceptable but critically desirable. Moreover, literature was attracting many more interested followers from the middle and even working classes who would have found Renaissance drama to be refreshingly revolutionary in spirit. The unorthodoxy that before had secluded Marlowe from critical inspection helped him to thrive in Lamb's work as one of the most fiery examples of the "Age of Shakespeare."

Yet, a closer look at Lamb's critical glosses indicates that even though a certain amount of moral unorthodoxy was permissible, certain elements of Marlowe's works and life had to be excerpted and reappropriated even in this adventurous critical work. While obviously trying to draw attention to the passions of Marlowe's characters and the emotional intensity of his poetry, Lamb's treatment of the playwright's life is short and·inaccurate.

> Marlowe is said to have been tainted with atheistical positions, to have denied God and the Trinity. To such a genius the history of Faustus must have been delectable food.[21]

This image of Marlowe as a skeptical epicure is understated in light of the well-known accounts that held that Marlowe was a foul-mouthed heretic and a lascivious murderer. Therefore, by privileging textual excerpts from Marlowe's plays and diminishing the importance of certain other published and accessible reports of Marlowe's life, Lamb was also able to distance himself from the playwright's reputation.

Moreover, even though his selections from Marlowe's plays seem extravagant and transgressive, Lamb, in fact, exposed his readers to these passages with the understanding that excellent poetry has certain passionate and amorphous qualities that transcend the often immoral and corrupt characteristics of the plays. For instance, Lamb provides a note in response to the Queen's lustful solicitations of the Moor in which he says

> The lines in the Extract [from *Lust's Dominion*] have a luscious smoothness in them, and they were the most temperate which I could pick out of this Play.[22]

Here he is actually apologizing for the subject matter of the excerpt while drawing attention to the poetic quality of the verse rather than to the actions of the Queen.

This tendency to deemphasize the subject matter is even more apparent in Lamb's consideration of *Tamburlaine,* a play in which a peasant hero encourages revolt and murder against existing regimes merely for the love of power. Lamb states that the lunes of Tamburlaine are perfect "midsummer madness." Then he provides an excerpt of "fine poetry" from a work from which, he confesses, he had trouble "culling a few sane lines."[23] The two selections from

Tamburlaine indeed provide representative examples of the work's refinement and its "madness" but little about its plot or theme (see appendix C).[24] Thus Lamb dismisses what he sees as Marlowe's excessive or mad poetic theme without having to draw attention to the radical (and, in fact, revolutionary) nature of the play's action. Therefore, his readers are not exposed to Tamburlaine's chaotic world view because Lamb, as the critic, has exercised full interpretive control of Tamburlaine's discourse.[25]

Similarly, Lamb responds to Barabas's outrages in *The Jew of Malta* by saying that the character

> is a mere monster brought in with a large painted nose to please the rabble. He kills in sport, poisons whole nunneries, invents infernal machines. He is just such an exhibition as a century or two earlier might have been played before the Londoners, *by the Royal command*, when a general pillage and massacre of the Hebrews had been previously resolved on in the cabinet. The idea of the Jew (which our pious ancestors contemplated with such horror) has nothing in it now revolting.[26]

Lamb steers the reader's attention, by way of these remarks, from the outrageous acts committed by both the Jew and the Christians in the play. By suggesting that Marlowe was artistically bound to an archaic but conventional way of representing the Jew, Lamb circumvents the idea that the play is yet another example of the brutal insensitivity of its author. Although most modern-day critics would agree with Lamb on this particular observation, his interpretation of the play should nonetheless be viewed as part of a general circumlocutionary strategy designed to elevate the appraisal of Marlowe's works.

Lamb ends his discussion of Marlowe with an observation concerning the nature of art that suggests that immoral acts are often portrayed in drama for essentially moral purposes. Speaking of Marlowe's portrayal of immoral characters such as Barabas and Faustus, Lamb says

> the holiest minds have sometimes not thought it blameable to counterfeit impiety in the person of another, to bring Vice in upon the stage speaking her own dialect, and, themselves being armed with an Unction of self-confident impunity, have not scrupled to handle and touch that familiarly, which would be death to others. Milton, in the person of Satan has started speculations hardier than any which the feeble armoury of the atheist ever

furnished: and the precise strait-laced Richardson has strengthened Vice, from the mouth of Lovelace, with entangling sophistries and abstruse pleas against her adversary Virtue which Sedley, Villiers, and Rochester, wanted depth of Libertinism sufficient to have invented.[27]

Along with aligning Marlowe with other prestigious names in poetry and drama, Lamb also holds that the immoral behavior found in Marlovian drama, although horrid, is not gratuitous but there to be exposed and condemned. This observation, which has since become a critical commonplace in Marlowe studies, was necessary before the playwright could be allowed any significant rank in the canon of Renaissance dramatists. Lamb's critical method, in this case, was extremely beneficial to Marlowe's reception because it made the playwright attractive to readers unstudied in non-Shakespearean drama, and it also provided a way of saying positive things about Marlowe without seeming to approve of various immoralities that were associated with his life and works. Lamb's assessment of the playwright, therefore, while not immediately influential, provided morally safe interpretive grounds on which later critics could stand when evaluating the playwright.

Other Play Collections and the Appearance of *Faustus*

Regardless of Lamb's recognition of Marlowe's achievement and the obvious esteem he had for the playwright's poetic capability, Marlowe's rise would not occur until the literary precepts of the prior century were broken down by the expansion of the publishing industry and by the new populism in the theater. Lamb's work, however, may have helped to renew an interest in the Dodsley format. An old plays collection reappeared in 1810 with the publication of *The Ancient British Drama* (this series is thought to have been edited by Walter Scott).[28] The editor includes both *Edward II* and *The Jew of Malta* but again fails to mention Marlowe among those he considers to be second- and even third-tier playwrights.

It must be recollected, that, besides the immortal Shakspeare, there flourished, during this period, Beaumont and Fletcher, Jonson, Ford, Massinger, and Webster; and the lesser, yet respectable names of Shirley, Daniel, Brome, Marston, Dekkar, and others, adorn the same age.[29]

Although this omission seems to suggest the relative obscurity of Marlowe's work in the critical mainstream during this period, one suspects that the editor may still have been reluctant to admit any specific appreciation for the playwright.

Baker's *Biographia Dramatica* of 1812 repeated Wood's account of Marlowe's atheism (which is duly condemned), yet credit is given to his poetic merit.[30] At this time, therefore, Marlowe's continuing obscurity may have been caused by the fact that his reputation still made him the unmentionable "other" who could not be considered openly by a conservative literary community.

Much more direct attention was given to Marlowe's work in the next decade (1810–20) than ever before. Because some guarded praise was given to *Faustus*, one wonders whether or not English men of letters had begun to realize that Goethe's legendary drama may have been in part influenced by the work of an English writer. In 1820, Collier notes that it "is well known that the greatest living poet of Germany has constructed a tragedy upon the same story [Faustus]."[31] In an environment where poets and other men of letters were attempting to elevate the respectability of the English literary tradition, the ability to claim that a great German poet may have been influenced by an English playwright would have made the editing and distribution of *Faustus* a priority. Also the fact that Marlowe used a German story to blend profound philosophical speculations with comic stage spectacles would have attracted the early nineteenth-century literati. During this period many poets and critics, influenced by Schiller, Hegel, and others, were adopting the ideology of German romantic philosophy,[32] and the "low" German melodrama had been imported for years in the theater, primarily with the translations of Kotzebue.

Indeed, there seems to have been some expanded interest in *Faustus* during the second decade of the nineteenth century. In a series that copied Dodsley's format, Charles Wentworth Dilke omitted *Edward II* and *The Jew of Malta* and instead printed only *Faustus* (this was, excluding William Mountfort's adaptation of the play in 1697, the first edition since 1663).[33] Henry Maitland ventured to compare Faustus to Lord Byron's Manfred, yet later, after receiving criticism, clarified his point by stating that "the mixed, rambling, headlong, and reckless manner of Marlow, in that Play, must not be put into competition with the sustained dignity of Byron."[34] Finally, even Coleridge, whose exclusive interest in Shakespeare made it rare for him to address a poet of Marlowe's standing, admitted being "familiar" with *Faustus*. Yet it seems as if this admission was only to establish that it was not Goethe's *Faust* that inspired his "old Michael Scott."[35] Generally the play was considered to have some historical importance, but it would not gain any widespread critical appreciation until the 1860s.

The 1825–27 Collier edition of Dodsley returned to the original selections of Marlowe, leaving *Faustus* out.[36] (The play would return in another 1830 series entitled *Old Enligsh Plays*.) At this point in the history of publishing it is obvious that the old plays were being repackaged more frequently into "new" editions. Thirty-six years divided the first (1744) and second (1780) editions of the *Old Plays*, and roughly the same amount of time between the second and third editions. Yet, in the next fifteen years, the Dodsley format was reproduced, with alterations in the types of plays, by both Dilke and Collier. The Dodsley format and other serial publications, comprised as they were of works that were quickly edited or reproduced from early quartos or from current theater prompt books, were seemingly being reproduced more for the easy profit than for antiquarian interests.

Indeed, the popular market for the plays is evinced, in some cases, by the fact that many were reproduced and sold shortly after a public performance. For instance, in 1818, William Oxberry, a fairly popular comedian on the hurly-burly London theater circuit, began producing a series of "new" English plays. This series, which seems to have been a sideline to Oxberry's acting career, was advertised as having "stage business" from recent productions as part of the texts. These plays were quickly edited and released at the rate of two plays a month.[37] Because many individual plays were seemingly reproduced from theater copies, they could be purchased for far less than Dodsley's volumes. Dodsley's monopoly on the old play series, therefore, was undermined by the appearance of new series, which more or less mass produced single old plays in a highly profitable and less expensive serial format.

Oxberry, who was the renowned author of "The History of Pugilism, and Memoirs of Persons who have distinguished themselves in that Science," was also an actor, an editor, a printer, and for a short and unsuccessful period, a theater manager. While these accomplishments do not further our interest in him here, he was the first person to edit and print all of Marlowe's plays. Eventually, he collected and edited a series of Marlowe's works into one volume.

Although Marlowe's work appeared repeatedly in the format of the old play series, there is little to suggest that his status was changed to any great extent in the literary community. What does seem likely is that these literary editors and publishers realized that the old plays could be packaged and sold in any number of formats, including Oxberry's. This new facet of the publishing industry, therefore, made Marlowe's plays more accessible to people outside of the strict confines of the society of learned literary critics and book collectors.

Changes in the Theater

Another change that affected the reception of Marlowe took place as a result of a much larger movement that subverted the polite and fashionable atmosphere of the eighteenth-century theater. One could say in fact that in the opening decades of the nineteenth century the theater was marked by a new and notorious public activism. According to Michael Booth, London grew in size from about nine hundred thousand to nearly three million by 1850, a fact that eventually led to an entirely different type of theater audience, one comprising mainly the working instead of the middle classes. Booth also notes that minor theaters were increasingly allowed by City authorities to play illicit dramas as long as they were "disguised" as burlettas, pantomines, or any other form of musical. This, along with massive demographic changes, led to "new patterns of patronage, taste and drama" that challenged the monopolies of the old patent theater.[38] These monopolies were further challenged both by the rising popularity of the opera among the moneyed classes, and by an odd and inimical form of class action against the raising of theater ticket prices among the poor. In 1809 the famous O.P. (old price) riots, which broke out in protest of raised admissions, also demonstrated the importance and the frequency of theater attendance among the working classes. By the second decade of the nineteenth century, theater performances had become more of a populist event with the increase of ticket buyers who were made up less of the aristocracy, beau monde, and middle-class, and more of the "gallery" class of poor spectators who could not afford tickets in the boxes and the pit.

The new presence of competitive minor theaters was also influential in changing radically the nature of theatrical performances at both Drury Lane and Covent Garden. Soon the major theaters, which had undergone renovation and expansion in the last decade of the eighteenth century, were in major financial difficulty. Theater managers like John Philip Kemble began relying more and more on sensational stage spectacles, which blended well with the crowd-pleasing melodrama and the low comedy that had become the staple of the London stage.[39] Also, the bad acoustics of the enlarged major theaters, coupled with the unruliness of the crowd, made high-minded renditions of great speeches almost impossible. The theater, therefore, had gone through a massive change not only in the way new plays were produced but in the manner in which old plays were revised to command the attention of a generally less sophisticated audience.

The Jew and Other Outsiders in Drama

In 1818 a greatly altered version of *The Jew of Malta* was revived, with Edmund Kean playing Barabas. Although the specific reasons for this production are unknown, something may be gathered from speculating about the treatment of the Jew in drama during this period, and also about the vogue for hero/villains among the playgoers of the day. The population expansion in London included, by the end of the eighteenth century, the arrival of twenty thousand Jews from the Continent, most of whom were destitute.[40] This demographic change, and the presence of actual impoverished Jews on the London streets, may have had something to do with the undermining of the symbolically evil Jew played by Macklin and Garrick in the eighteenth century. At any rate, the subject of the Jew in drama was becoming popular, it seems, for reasons more sentimental than anti-Semitic.[41]

A play by Richard Cumberland called simply *The Jew* took up the subject of the common anti-Semitic preconceptions held by the middle class.[42] The plot of the play, however, revolves around the fact that the Jewish hero, Sheva, who is treated unkindly by the distrusting Christians, turns out to be benevolent and kindly. *The Jew* was a popular production that was printed and reprinted in multiple editions through the early nineteenth century. Furthermore, in 1814, Kean changed Shylock by playing him with a black instead of a red wig in a production of *The Merchant of Venice* that was highly successful. It seems that instead of being portrayed as the stereotypical red-haired "evil Jew," Shylock was represented as the dark but tragically misunderstood outsider. The early nineteenth-century stage was known in fact for producing heroes who, like Sheva and Shylock, were either socially misunderstood or villain/outsiders, marginalized by society. Perhaps this is one of the reasons that *Othello* and *Richard III* also remained popular throughout this era.

The year 1818 was also the year of *Frankenstein*, a work that was part of a renewal of the Gothic form. Here the monster/outsider is again forced into villainy by bigotry and paranoia. The social implications of the popularity of monster types, which include Maturin's *Melmoth*, has been discussed by Marilyn Butler, who holds that

> *Frankenstein* and *Melmoth* are intended as attacks on the current alliance between conservative politics and High Church or Catholic religion, they revive the conscious liberalism of Gothic in the 1790's, and run counter to the strongest trend in immediately contemporary Romantic writing from the Continent.[43]

The populist bias toward dark heroes, therefore, may have been rooted in this anti–high church and antiromantic sentiment. Moreover, in the theaters the largely working-class audience (who were perhaps put off by pretentious displays of classical virtues) identified with the tortured hero who, because of his physical difference, becomes a psychological outsider. This Gothic vogue seems to have inspired the first production of a Marlovian drama in well over one hundred years.

Kean and Oxberry

Although not all the rumors about Kean's itinerant upbringing and his physical deformity are creditable, one report in the usually reliable *Dictionary of National Biography* holds that Kean, at one point during his youth, had his education financed for a period by a rich Jewish merchant. Whether or not this is true, it seems that he had every reason to identify with the marginalized and oppressed numbers of a growing industrial society, whether they were Jewish or not.

In 1818, Kean evidently played down some of the more anti-Semitic characteristics of Barabas in a bowdlerized version of *The Jew of Malta* by Samson Penley. The production was altered for what seems to be the specific purpose of lessening the impact of Barabas's cruelty. Although the play received "interested" reviews, it was acted only twelve times. The significance of this fairly minor production at Drury Lane is seen in the way it was received in the resolutely conservative *Blackwood's Magazine*.

> We cannot agree with many persons in thinking, that this play is without a moral purpose; or that Barabas is a mere monster [see Lamb 27], and not a man. We cannot allow, that even Ithamore is gratuitously wicked. There is no such thing in nature—least of all in human nature, and Marlow knew this. It is true that Ithamore appears to be so at first sight. He finds it a pleasant pastime to go about and kill men and women who have never injured him. But it must not be forgotten that he is a slave; and a slave should no more be expected to keep a compact with the kind from which he is cut off, than a demon or a wild beast.[44]

This production, at least in the mind of this reviewer, must have affirmed his politically suspect view of the inherent verities of human nature. His kinship with the "Marlowe" whom he conjured from an extremely altered production is, as well, a vivid example of how a critic can interpret an "author signifier" in any way he sees fit. This type of ideological appropriation is typical of how Marlowe was treated by critics throughout the rest of the nineteenth century.[45]

Also in 1818, Oxberry decided to collect and edit all of Marlowe's plays at roughly the same time that Kean revived *The Jew of Malta*, thus making affordable separate editions of Marlowe's work available to the general public. And it seems from these two events that Marlowe's works were becoming a much more "public" concern. According to a then current anecdote, Oxberry and Edmund Kean were friends.[46] Whether or not they were, it is certain that Marlowe, by 1820, had been exposed to a much broader readership and audience than was afforded by the Dodsley series. This exposure, furthermore, was achieved through the efforts of Oxberry, the hack editor, who was mass producing prompt books, and Kean, the tragic actor/outsider, who seemed bent on rectifying the image of the Jew in society. Both men lived on the theatrical margins of a rapidly expanding industrial economy.

Hazlitt's *Lectures*

Although early nineteenth-century critical perspectives on the age of Elizabeth were influenced by a romantic bias, a close inspection of the dramatic criticism of such literary figures as Lamb, Hazlitt, and Hunt indicates that each critic had a distinctly different approach to reviving old drama. Thus the understanding that each of these critics had of Marlowe, although they were literary associates whose work was no doubt informed by the literary spirit of the times, cannot be grouped under a general romantic sentiment. Lamb's urbane and seemingly apolitical presentation of Marlovian specimens in 1808 is far different from Hazlitt's contemplative and politically contentious inspection of the playwright's work over ten years later. Moreover, Hunt's sponsorship of R. H. Horne's radical dramatic rendition of Marlowe's death in 1830 and his sensational views of the playwright's work in 1844 owe little to any established critical precedents concerning Marlowe.

Therefore, each critic has received separate treatment in this study. In terms of their views on drama, Lamb and Hazlitt apparently wrote for what was, in the early nineteenth century, a growing body of open-minded middle-class readers who were generally interested in the theater, old and new. Horne and Hunt, however, are presented in chapter 4 as predecessors of a movement that established Marlowe's life and works as an exemplary challenge to certain Victorian values.

When determining exactly what effect such critics as Lamb, Hazlitt, and Hunt had on the early nineteenth-century revival of Marlowe, certain historical matters should be made clear. First of all, these men, while they appreciated Marlowe's work much more than did their critical predecessors, only considered the playwright within the much wider context of old drama. Moreover, their views did not contribute to any widespread acknowledgement of the playwright's talents until they were recalled years later by several influential Victorian critics.

Even after these qualifications have been made, however, one must admit that Lamb, Hazlitt, and, as we shall see later, Horne and Hunt shared a romantic fascination with the passionate and imaginative features of Marlowe's life and works, which boosted the playwright's popularity. The first strong acknowledgment of Marlowe's importance was expressed by Hazlitt in his *Lectures on the Age of Elizabeth* (1820).[47] Originally part of a series of lectures given at the Surrey Institution, Hazlitt's views on Marlowe boldly departed from the standard critical habit of ignoring the playwright and in fact a large body of non-Shakespearean drama. Instead Hazlitt celebrates the vigorous and innovative spirit of the work of Shakespeare's contemporaries among whom he ranked Marlowe the highest, and he bemoans the fact that the playwrights Webster, Decker, Marston, Marlowe, Chapman, Heywood, Middleton, and Rowley had been lost to antiquity.

> They went out one by one unnoticed, like evening lights' or were swallowed up in the headlong torrent of puritanic zeal which succeeded, and swept away every thing in its unsparing course, throwing up the wrecks of taste and genius at random, and at long fitful intervals, amidst the painted gew-gaws and foreign frippery of the reign of Charles II, and from which we are only now recovering the scattered fragments and broken images to erect a temple to true Fame![48]

Hazlitt's praise of Shakespeare's contemporaries befitted the characteristically untraditional attitudes of his audience at the Surrey Institution, comprised, as David Bromwich notes, "of the self-taught and the self-improving: middle class. . . . many of them Dissenters or Quakers."[49]

Echoing Dodsley's bias toward the accomplishments of indigenous dramatists, Hazlitt explicitly states that Elizabethan authors "had something in them that savoured of the soil from which they grew: they were not French, they were not Dutch, or German, or Greek, or Latin; they were truly English."[50] This statement is made after Hazlitt asserts that Englishmen have undervalued their past. Although this idea may not seem strongly reformist to us, Hazlitt is directing an attack on certain conservative critics who persisted in dismissing Elizabethan drama on the grounds that it was formally unrefined and philosophically unsophisticated. Therefore, his observations on the inherent genius of English writers whom he wished to save from obscurity are not, as they may seem, ardently patriotic. They are instead contentious reflections from a dissenter dismayed by the lack of imaginative thinking and intellectual openess in English society. Butler further notes that

> His [Hazlitt's] criticism proper belongs to the liberal new wave of 1816–19; even the restless, sceptical, self-tormenting and doubting essays are rooted in an individualism which goes back to Dissent and always retains its idiosyncratic critical posture, its rational and activist potential. Because Hazlitt matured so late, when the English liberal-intellectual renaissance of the post-war years was effectively in retreat, his oeuvre is that of an isolated no-sayer driven by unpropitious circumstances into himself, and into wholly notional opposition.[51]

Hazlitt's contemplative and sometimes brooding reflections on old dramatists support this description of his later work. In a typically republican fashion, he finds the Elizabethans "bold, vigorous, independent" thinkers who had been ignored by a society too "dazzled with the gloss and novelty of modern discoveries" and too quick to reject the uninhibited expressions of past cultures as barbaric and ignorant.[52]

This observation exemplifies the spirit of liberal reform that typifies Hazlitt's role not only as a critic but as a lecturer. (Bromwich also notes that a "lecturer" in the nineteenth century was often a "minister who had lost his complacency."[53]) In these lectures, in fact, he seems to reveal more personal rancor than political activism. One can, in fact, find a parallel between what Hazlitt perceives as a general disrespect during his time not only for the achievements of the Elizabethans but for the reformist movement with which he was involved during the 1790s.

> Instead of letting them [the old playwrights] reflect any lustre, or add any credit to the period of history to which they rightfully belong, we only make use of their example to insult and degrade it still more beneath our own level.[54]

Although this observation on the English dramatists seems to testify to Hazlitt's cultural chauvinism, it actually reflects what he saw as his own political estrangement from English society during the early decades of the nineteenth century. In essence, Hazlitt is not praising English achievements of the past as much as he is condemning conservatives, in front of an audience largely comprising the "radical" middle class, for rejecting the spirit of individualism both in old drama and in the type of liberal reform for which he had fought.

Hazlitt elevates the work of Marlowe and his contemporaries, therefore, seemingly to play out the drama of his struggle against conservatism. The fact that Hazlitt evaluates *Faustus* first and foremost among Marlowe's works, for example, signals an idiosyncratic critical perspective. While calling the play a "rude sketch," he seems overwhelmed by the sublimity and emotional power of many individual scenes.[55] One may recall that Thomas Warton, who roughly forty years before had been one of the early defenders of Marlowe, considered *Faustus* only as proof of the ignorance that "still prevailed" in Elizabethan times. Hazlitt, though, is fascinated by the central theme of the play.

> Faustus, in his impatience to fulfill at once and for a moment, for a few short years, all the desires and conceptions of his soul, is willing to give in exchange his soul and body to the great enemy of mankind.[56]

Hazlitt therefore shared with his "romantic" contemporaries a philosophical fascination with examples of the irreverent and diabolical in the literature of the past. However, the "great enemy of mankind," in Hazlitt's view, has perhaps more political resonance than the Lucifer of old.

For instance, when describing Marlowe, whose poetry he likens to Faustus's necromancy, Hazlitt evokes an amazing picture not of the late sixteenth but of the early nineteenth century.

> There is a lust of power in his writings, a hunger and thirst after unrighteousness, a glow of the imagination, unhallowed by any thing but its own energies. His thoughts burn within him like a furnace with bickering flames; or throwing out black smoke and mist that hide the dawn of genius, or like a poisonous mineral, corrode the heart.[57]

By drawing a parallel between Marlowe's writing and Faustus's magic, Hazlitt uses images of industry to describe things evil and demonic. The furnace with "bickering flames," the "black smoke and mist," the poison and corrosion are all images that bring to mind industrial expansion and a Faustian underworld simultaneously. By saying that the "dawn of genius," in Marlowe's work, is hidden by smoke and corrosion, Hazlitt suggests as well that these curiously industrial images are in fact in conflict not only with a higher poetical but a higher social consciousness.

Hazlitt's essays during this period, even delivered as they were to a public forum, seem to mark his retreat from political dissent into a world of books and reflections. His emphasis on the Promethean energy that *Faustus* resounds is typical of a free thinker who had been schooled politically in the republican fervor of the early 1790s. His dark understanding of Marlowe and *Faustus*, though, may be in some contentious way directed at what he sees as the Faustian trade of social sensibility for industrial expansion. If so, then the reappearance of *Faustus* in English letters may owe something to the fact that it was appropriated, by Hazlitt, as a metaphor for the unrighteous exchange of culture for the marvels of the machine age.

The 1826 Pickering Edition

If it had been possible for one to purchase stock in Marlowe in 1817, the securities would have paid off well by the 1826 appearance of his complete works, published by a respectable printer. William Pickering, who had formerly been the printer of Cicero, Chaucer, Boccaccio, and Johnson, put together a three-volume collection of Marlowe's *Works*.[58] The fact that Marlowe's value had increased is apparent by the attractiveness of the edition, which sold for 27s. By this time, the only other "second tier" sixteenth- and early seventeenth-century playwrights who had complete editions of their works in print were Marston, Chapman, Ford, and Massinger (only Ford and Massinger were printed contemporaneously with Marlowe's works). So, if a complete edition of a writer's collected works issued by a reputable publisher is any indication of a writer's perceived value, then Marlowe, who had before been only a subject for literary coteries, was by the mid-1820s considered a substantial Renaissance literary figure.

Finally, a strong indication of the new valuation of Marlowe can be found in the unsigned preface of the Pickering edition, probably written by the editor, George Robinson, which reveals how the image of Marlowe had been improved by an essentialist, as well as manipulative, critical methodology. The writer notes that Marlowe was the only pre-Shakespearean poet to make "an impression upon the hearts of the audience." He also contends that Marlowe "drew his materials from a purer source" than many of his contemporaries, and that he was the first "to adopt a more natural and chaste model" for his drama.[59] The emphasis on abstract terms like the heart, purity, chastity, and nature was a critical fashion of the times, yet what is important is that Marlowe has gone through a complete metamorphosis. As late as 1810, he was the debauched atheist whose poetry showed some talent but was basically unrefined. By the 1820s, he began to exhibit those poetic qualities which early nineteenth-century poets and critics so loved in themselves. Of Marlowe's personal reputation, the writer enthusiastically states that the playwright

> . . . has been equally the subject of high panegyric, and the sport of scurrilous abuse, esteemed for his verse and hated for his life, the favorite of the learned and witty, and the horror of the precise and religious. The praise applies to his intellectual and the censure to his moral character; what the latter really was may be difficult at this time to determine with accuracy, although the accusations are not of a nature to be entitled to any great weight.[60]

The fact that much of this biographical polemic could have been easily used to defend the lives of either Shelley or Byron indicates that the textual accounts of Marlowe's personal life were now being placed aside on the grounds that hard evidence was lacking and that poetic genius excuses personal intemperance. The writer of the preface conclusively states that "Marlowe's familiar appellative was Kit, which may be considered as evidence of a kind disposition, or a companionable nature."[61] Indeed, as the title page to the expensive first volume refers to "Kit" Marlowe's *Works*, it is certain that the playwright's debut into nineteenth-century literary society is imminent.

Marlowe's status grew in the opening decades of the nineteenth century, therefore, because of several simultaneous events. First, literary critics such as Lamb and Hazlitt developed sound ways to present Marlowe to a growing body of interested middle-class readers. It is important to note that both Lamb and Hazlitt avoided any direct discussion of what was then known about the playwright's biography. Also, through the advent of an open marketplace for copies of theater prompt books and the public desire to be entertained by the monstrous villains of melodrama, Marlowe gained a public forum. On a slightly higher plane, too, Marlowe was the subject of debate in several of the newly formed periodicals of the period. The critical attention given to Marlowe, however, initially had less influence on the playwright's growing status than his appearance on the theater circuit and in certain reviews. Because of this public exposure, Marlowe's works became more salable in a market that was realizing the growing financial potentials of recycled old authors. Moreover, as demonstrated by the Pickering editor, his new popularity won him defenders from a variety of critical persuasions throughout the rest of the nineteenth century.

2
The Foundations of Marlowe Scholarship

In his 1969 edition, J. B. Steane suggests that there was once a consensus concerning the features of Marlowe's life and personality. "There was a time not so very long ago," says Steane, "when literary gentlemen could meet, say 'Christopher Marlowe' to each other, and be fairly sure that they were going to talk about the same person." Steane continues by arguing that, while much valuable research had been done in roughly the three decades before his edition, the field had become jaded by random and irresponsible speculations that were expressed "most forcibly," he asserts, "in the universities of the United States." Steane's edition is still a standard classroom text that has been reprinted over a dozen times through the 1970s and 1980s.[1]

While it is true that interpretations of Marlowe's life and work took more radical and dispersed courses in the 1960s, there was never any solid biographical foundation from which to diverge. From the rediscovery of the playwright in the early nineteenth century until the current date, scholars have had to rely mostly on random secondary reports, some of which came from the time around Marlowe's death and some of which originated many years later. There are, for instance, crucial misconceptions of Marlowe's life that arose in the nineteenth century and that have been perpetuated by critics to this day. The only consistent feature of Marlowe scholarship is that his life, from the time that it was reassembled in the nineteenth century until the current date, has been subjected to various and often widely conflicting interpretations. Moreover, these disparities originated in the 1820s, not in the 1960s, and long before any investigation of Marlowe's life and work took place in the United States.

By the mid-1820s the old obscure and reprehensible Marlowe had been transformed into a new and powerful literary figure whose works were becoming the subject of serious research. Whereas the scholarship of non-Shakesperean Renaissance literature had previously been conducted by dedicated connoisseurs and hobbyists, the second quarter of the nineteenth century saw the advent of a new type of research scholar—one who was far more the archaeologist than the collector in that he was more exact and methodical. This chapter will cover the discoveries of three Victorian researchers who began an extensive review of forgotten and ignored manuscripts and play quartos in order to establish the essential features of Marlowe's biography. Although they were not the pure literary professionals one finds in the later part of the century, James Broughton, John Payne Collier, and Alexander Dyce were surprisingly dedicated and accurate. Indeed, by 1850 most of the groundwork for modern Marlowe scholarship had been laid by these men.

Much of what they found from roughly 1820 to 1850, however, was ignored, overlooked, or distorted in some way by historians, teachers, and critics who were pressed by larger theoretical or ideological concerns. Furthermore, there were even critical points at which these early researchers were unable to remain objective themselves. The period between the first and second Pickering editions of Marlowe's works (that is, between 1826 and 1850), while it produced meticulous and substantial documentation of the playwright's life, left a legacy of uncertainty and misrepresentation. From its beginning, it seems Marlowe scholarship was doomed to be muddled by bias, conjecture, oversight, and even forgery.

James Broughton and the Puritans

In August of 1819 a reviewer of Nathan Drake's *Shakspeare and his Times* suggested that Christopher Marlowe was probably a *nom de guerre* "assumed for a time" by Shakespeare.[2] Roughly one year later, in the same journal, a reviewer of Hazlitt's *Lectures on Elizabethan Poetry* concluded that there was now no doubt that Marlowe was "but a borrowed designation of the great Shakespeare."[3] This theory was not taken seriously enough to have any lasting effect on Marlowe studies, but it did reveal several important features of what was then the state of literary research. First, there was a strong tendency in the early nineteenth century to view the English literary Renaissance only in terms of Shakespeare's isolated achievements. The specific suggestion that Marlowe was in fact only an alter ego of Shakespeare further indicates that some critics wished to form a literary history around the singular achievements of a few great men (an impulse that is still strong in the curricula today). While we may see the argument for Shakespeare's authorship of Marlowe's plays as being ridiculously unsophisticated and conjectural, there was no solid scholarship at that time with which one could reject such an assertion concerning Marlowe. There were in fact no documents that proved beyond reasonable doubt that Marlowe indeed had ever existed.

James Broughton's contribution to Marlowe scholarship, although not prolific, represented the first successful attempt in the nineteenth century to clarify and challenge the reports of Marlowe's life. In a series of monthly articles printed in the *Gentleman's Magazine* (1830), he systematically sought to set the record straight with a precision that much criticism lacks even to this day.[4] His efforts to clear Marlowe's bad name, while colored by his apparent disgust with moralistic condemnations of the theater both in the sixteenth century and during his own time, were for the most part accurate and reliable. While students and critics have since come to expect—however rightly—Broughton's type of objectivity from literary scholars in this century, the high quality of his literary research was rare for his time.

In 1826 the editor of the Pickering edition, Robinson, attempted to defend Marlowe by maintaining that certain evidence that damaged the playwright's reputation should not be given any "great weight."[5] While Broughton agreed with this statement, he thought that it lacked convincing bibliographical support. According to him, the entire preface "slurred over with a provoking degree of carelessness" the events of Marlowe's life and times.[6] Broughton goes on to report what was the accepted knowledge of the day concerning Marlowe after he quips about the ill-documented nature of prior reports.

> The current tale respecting him [Marlowe], which the compiler of every biographical dictionary and cyclopedia has been content to copy from his immediate predecessor with confiding carelessness, is this:—that he was born about 1562; was entered of Benet Coll. Cambridge, where he took the degrees of B.A. 1583, and M.A. 1587; that on quitting the University he repaired to London, became a celebrated actor and dramatist, ran a dissolute career, published some blasphemous works oppugning the doctrine of the Trinity, and lost his life at last "in a lewd quarrel," either with Ben Jonson or "a baudie servingman," about a harlot.[7]

While some of its details originated during the time of Marlowe's death, this resume had had much added to it over the years. For instance, that Marlowe was an actor, that his murderer and rival in love was either Ben Jonson or a pimp of some sort, and that Marlowe died in a tavern, were "facts" included by biographers many years after his death. Other matters, too, had been distorted or embellished by historians who could not resist the temptation to sensationalize Marlowe's murder. The common assumption that the playwright was provoked into a duel over a serving woman was derived from Francis Meres's *Palladis Tamia* (1598), wherein Meres states that "as the poet Lycophron was shot to death by a certain rival of his: so Christopher Marlowe was stabbed to death by a bawdy serving man, a rivall of his in his lewde love."[8] This report began the saga of the Light Woman mentioned again by Wood and, although strongly challenged by Broughton, basically repeated by historiographers and critics until Leslie Hotson's breakthrough in the 1920s.[9]

This type of mythmaking frustrated Broughton, who protested that the reports of the lover, the rival, and the blasphemer were not necessarily valid:

> the reader, who has doubtless often seen this libel confidently detailed in the "Biographia Dramatica," and books of that stamp will be surprised to learn that every circumstance here related of Marlowe, is, to say the least, uncertain, save that of being a popular writer, and being slain in a broil, which, however, was neither with Ben Jonson, nor about a wench.[10]

Broughton's confidence here is rooted in an important discovery he had made some ten years before this report.

During his research, Broughton noticed that a reference to Marlowe made by William Vaughan in a work entitled *The Golden Grove* (1600) mentioned Deptford as the location of Marlowe's death. Using this information, Broughton, in 1820, petitioned the parson of St. Nicholas, Deptford, to examine the church burial register.[11] There it was recorded that Christopher Marlowe was slain on 1 June 1593, thus giving some substance to the account of his early and violent death (the parson misread the name of the person who killed Marlowe as being Francis Archer instead of Ingram Friser, a mistake that would delay further discovery concerning the matter for over one hundred years).[12] Not only did Broughton find the first piece of solid evidence concerning Marlowe's death, he located and questioned the validity of other spurious documents, opening a debate over several essential features of Marlowe's life. Specifically, he called into question the birthdate given by the eighteenth-century scholar Edmond Malone; he examined the records at Benet College, Cambridge, and questioned Marlowe's enrollment there;[13] and finally, he challenged the belief that Marlowe was an actor.

Although most of Broughton's observations turned out to be accurate, his research may have been driven by a desire not only to vindicate Marlowe but the playmaker in general. Moreover, he was implicitly defending not just the sixteenth-century stage but the early nineteenth-century theater against moral condemnations from religious conservatives. Broughton shows a thorough disgust with the opinions of religious extremists by dismissing Thomas Beard (who doomed Marlowe as an atheist in 1597) as a "fierce and vindictive Puritan."[14] He further ridicules Puritan chauvinism in general by saying that

> writers, who numbered among the deadly sins health-drinking, hair-curling, dancing, church-music, and, above all, playwriting, would scarcely fail (like many Puritans of our own day) to term the premature death of such a person a special manifestation of divine vengeance.[15]

The parenthetical parallel drawn here between sixteenth- and early nineteenth-century Puritans seems to be more the motive behind Broughton's argument than merely an isolated desire to defend Marlowe.

Later, as Broughton continues his diatribe against Puritanism, he quotes a current reviewer who claimed that the multitudes of nineteenth-century theatergoers "will look back with unutterable anguish on the nights and days in which the plays of Shakspeare ministered to their guilty delights." To this Broughton declares:

> Let him recollect of what extravagancies to this same spirit, sometimes dormant, but never extinct, has impelled men to the commission in our times, when the conflagration of one theatre has been styled from the pulpit a national blessing, and the sudden downfall of another described (in a strain of impious buffoonery) as the triumphant issue of a contest between the Deity and the Evil Principle for the possession of its site.[16]

These remarks are directed against a review entitled *The Ground of the Theatre* by George Charles Smith in which it was proposed that the ground of the New Brunswick Theatre, having been formerly occupied as a place of worship, be restored to its original state.[17] Here Broughton, by referring to a theater turned into a church, offers us an intriguing insight into what he saw as a competition between the two forums for public assembly during his time. Both church and theater provided space for workers to convene during their leisure time, and both had to solicit a financial base to maintain themselves. Conspicuously, in a biographical survey of Marlowe, Broughton pauses to defend the value of the theater against the "Puritans," who saw it not only as a place where Christian values were threatened but as an enterprise with which the Church competed for both physical space and disposable income.

Broughton also seems to suggest that nineteenth-century nonconformists attacked the theater more harshly than did even sixteenth-century Puritans. Other historians not only have supported this observation but have suggested that the collusion of old religious and new industrial values was to blame for the general feeling of hostility toward the theater among the pious. According to the Hammonds, the contempt that the Methodists had for the theater was rooted specifically in the fact that it encouraged social indolence and other behavior that opposed not only the will of God but the demands of industry as well.[18] What is important about Broughton's attack on the Puritans is that he was not only struggling to free a playwright from embellished puritanical reports of the sixteenth and early seventeenth centuries but also refuting religious intolerance of the theater in his own day.

The subtext of Broughton's defense of Marlowe, therefore, was that he was attempting to defend his own view of the theater. While he remained objective to a degree, his political motives tended to direct his discussion more than they should. For instance, Broughton follows the Pickering editor in questioning whether Marlowe was ever an actor because of the lack of sound evidence to support such an assumption. Later Broughton laconically asserts that "no proof whatever exists of his [Marlowe] having been an actor, though his biographers, drawing their inferences from the probability of the thing, have universally pronounced that it actually was the case." Broughton then cites what he believes to be the source of the misconception.

This erroneous supposition, that Marlowe was an actor, arose, I believe, from an equivocal expression made use of by Greene in his "Groat's-worth of Wit," where he styles him a "famous gracer of tragedians;" but at this period the words tragedian and comedian, which now seldom signify anything but actor, were commonly put for dramatist; and, in fact, a century after, they were still used in that sense.[19]

Broughton's observation here is valid, but the fact that he goes on at length about this matter in a relatively short article indicates that he wished to distance his subject from what, in his time, was considered a profession that often attracted flamboyant and depraved personalities.

Another reason that Broughton wished to distance Marlowe from what was often seen as an ignoble profession is that he was attempting to hold up the standard biographical treatment of Marlowe as yet another example of social injustice. Toward the end of his survey of Marlowe's life, he states that Marlowe's biographers have "dismissed poor Christopher to perdition, like his own Faustus, without troubling themselves to inquire into the justice of his sentence."[20] Later Broughton even parallels Marlowe's plight with that of a political reformer by flatly stating that the playwright was the "Tom Paine of the sixteenth century," because like Paine he was "ever before condemned upon testimony so completely unsupported by proof, and rendered to questionable by the reputation of the parties rendering it."[21] It cannot go unsaid that Broughton proposed a new image of Marlowe as a type of historical martyr. A sentimentalized version of this view of the playwright gained support from the playwright's most noteworthy admirers later in the century, although the original political implication of Broughton's observation was abstracted.

Although Broughton's republican leanings color his defense of Marlowe, he nonetheless successfully exposed the bogus nature of certain historical accounts he felt had been contaminated by Puritan biases. Moreover, Broughton's research was thorough; there was indeed no strong reason to believe that Marlowe had been an actor. Had it not been for Collier's later manipulations of certain records, Broughton's effort to provide a sound foundation for Marlowe scholarship may even have succeeded. Marlowe would return to the stage, however, both literally and figuratively, through the machinations of Collier, who, in order to illuminate Marlowe's raw talent, wished him to be an actor. In fact, Collier tampered with certain key features of Marlowe's life and work in ways from which interpretations of the playwright's achievement would never quite recover.

The Collier Era

While Broughton brought to the study of Marlowe more biographical objectivity, John Payne Collier (1789–1883) formed non-Shakesperean English drama into an entire literary field. His *History of English Dramatic Poetry* (1831), a landmark in the bibliography of literature, would not only establish him as the foremost expert on the history of English drama but would essentially change the nature of critical studies aimed at examining Shakespeare and English literary history.[22] Collier's interests in Marlowe's work were more far reaching than Broughton's because Collier, by affixing convincing dates to Marlowe's plays and by documenting the development of certain poetic and thematic features in pre-Shakespearean texts, allotted Marlowe a highly significant place within the entire history of English drama.

Essentially Collier was the first to establish Marlowe and his pre-Shakesperean peers as eclectics who brought together a variety of traditions from which Shakespeare could borrow. Although Broughton fended off certain naive assumptions about Marlowe's biography, there were still those who were simply offended by the constant hyperbole and rant of Marlowe's dramatic characters. By convincingly attributing the advent of blank verse on the popular stage to Marlowe, Collier placed the playwright in the position of being the most influential pre-Shakespearean. Therefore, he argued that the playwright's works were significant on grounds other than their overall dramatic merit. Unlike Broughton, however, whose accuracy was only slightly marred by certain religious and political biases, Collier was a relentless forger, whose compulsion to falsify documents mystifies scholars even to this day. On one hand, he was unprecedented in his ability to cross-reference various details in order to provide an accurate picture of the sequence of dramatic events that occurred in and around Shakespeare's time. On the other, he would stop at nothing to validate his findings.

Although Collier's contributions to literary study were immense,

they have been largely effaced from literary history because of the
reputation of his forgeries and falsifications. The widely scattered
legacy of bibliographical uncertainty that Collier left behind is intensified by the fact that his work was often accurate and insightful.
Because he was so able and because his falsifications were often
cleverly hidden, many questions concerning his claims are still dis-
puted. In this section, Collier's life and work will be examined in
order to determine exactly how and why Marlowe studies, when they
were becoming more reliable than ever before, became thoroughly
confused by seemingly random misrepresentations.

In a profession usually enjoyed by well-educated men who had
enough money to pursue the often profitless venture of literary research, Collier himself was the son of a failed entrepreneur who had
to resort to hack writing in order to feed his family. Instead of
continuing his schooling, the son followed his father's lead and became a parliamentary reporter. After a short and pretentious effort at
being a poet, Collier managed to establish a professional relationship
with Edward and Septimus Prowett, who ran a publishing house on
the Strand. In 1825 he was asked to edit the last six volumes of
Dodsley's *Old Plays*, thus finishing an aborted project begun by Septimus Prowett eleven years earlier. The price for the quickly edited
set was too high (five pounds) for editions that were replete with
proofing errors.[23] While it has been pointed out that Collier never had
a chance to examine the proofs, the series has become, for some, an
early testimony to its editor's questionable credibility. This third
edition of Dodsley is also of interest because Collier, by insisting that
four plays be added by the then obscure authors Lodge, Greene,
Nashe, and Peele, provides one of the first groupings of pre-Shakespearean dramatists.

It would not be until Collier's forgeries in the famous Perkins folio
were exposed in the late 1850s, however, that his reputation would be
questioned seriously. In the years before this disgrace, he overcame
his poverty and lack of schooling and became perhaps the most active
and well-received literary historian in England. One reason why
Collier's research was in many ways superior to scholars before and
after was that, because he had to resort to hack reviewing for income,
he gained a thorough understanding of actual theater production. His
bibliographical reasoning, therefore, was always historically sound.

He was also fortunate enough to gain unlimited access to certain key private play collections. He became acquainted with old drama as a teenager by examining the extensive Garrick collection in the British Museum. Soon Crabb Robinson introduced him to Thomas Amyot, who later arranged an introduction for Collier to William Cavendish, the sixth Duke of Devonshire and the proprietor of the most impressive private holdings of drama in England. Among the treasures of Devonshire's library was the collection of uncatalogued plays assembled by John Philip Kemble. Finally, Collier gained access, through Amyot, to the Alleyn papers at Dulwich College. There he was able to examine firsthand information that, previously, he could only cite from Malone's records. As it turned out, these collections made it possible for Collier to assemble the most thorough history of English drama that had ever been produced. Later, his research would be enriched to an even greater degree after he was allowed access to the Ellesmere manuscripts at the Bridgewater House library.[24]

Collier began his study of old plays during a time when far too little was known or understood about Shakespeare's dramatic predecessors and contemporaries. Therefore, he approached his research of Renaissance theater not as a servile archivist but with a conscious purpose to establish himself as the foremost authority of a new field—one that, by carefully documenting the rise of Shakespearean drama, also marked the advent of English cultural sensibility. To do this, he began by researching the non-Shakespearean elements of Renaissance drama and building an area of study that would provide substantial proof that Shakespearean drama was not an individual phenomenon but the peak of a collective and indigenous cultural movement.

In his *History of English Dramatic Poetry,* Collier echoes Dodsley by arguing that the English dramatic tradition was superior to the dramatic traditions of other nations and that it slowly developed poetic quality through time. Aside from asserting that English drama must be seen as a separate and distinct genre with its own history, Collier holds that Shakespearean drama should be read in the light of the influence of the dramatic styles and conventions of Shakespeare's predecessors, specifically those of Greene, Lyly, Peele, Nashe, Lodge, and, most prominently, Marlowe. Collier's history also puts forward several other critical observations that have become traditions in Marlowe scholarship. For instance, he traces the history of blank verse from its beginnings in the works of Surrey, and Norton and Sackville, to Marlowe, whom he argues was the first to use blank verse "in dramatic compositions performed in public theatre." He also draws connections between Marlowe's imagery and the playwright's possible sources in Spenser. Collier's observations in his history of English drama are ground-breaking, and his review of Marlowe makes much modern scholarship seem surprisingly unoriginal.[25]

After he had argued that the quality of English drama had developed from its medieval beginnings to Shakespeare, Collier in 1844 attempted to provide a definitive edition of Shakespeare securely placed as the pinnacle of Collier's literary-historical paradigm. This collaborative effort with Knight was generally well received, but there were critics, including Alexander Dyce, who harshly denounced the edition. Evidently, Collier was not satisfied with this partial success. In 1852 he reported that he had discovered a Shakespeare folio, dated 1632 and supposedly edited by a Thomas Perkins, that provided the answers to many of the key problems in Shakespeare's texts. (It included roughly thirty thousand marginal entries.) Because it confirmed so many of Collier's own emendations in his 1844 edition, the discovery immediately drew suspicion from Collier's peers, who, after several years, managed to prove that it was a fake. Although as a result Collier was completely exposed and disgraced, he never confessed to this or to many other forgeries that he committed during his career.[26]

Collier's lifelong effort to build Renaissance drama into a literary field, it seems, was supposed to have established him as the leading authority of Shakespeare and his age. The Perkins disaster, however, exposed Collier as a man who was profoundly and relentlessly driven by his professional ambition. Other forgeries, though, such as certain fabricated ballads,[27] make his efforts hard to explain solely as being the result of professional expediency. One is tempted to think therefore that Collier was not always in his right mind. However, his falsifications of Marlowe, like his forgeries of Shakespeare, follow a logical pattern when placed in the broader context of what he was trying to accomplish professionally.

Specifically, in order to emphasize Marlowe's important role in the development of drama, Collier tried to validate two important features of the playwright's life and work through forgery. First, he

attempted to prove beyond doubt that Marlowe was the author of
Tamburlaine and that he wrote it at the beginning of his career.
Second, he attempted to establish that Marlowe was an actor. Together, these features of Marlowe's life and work would show that the
same person who pioneered blank verse on the public stage had a
specific understanding of histrionics and staging. They would also
indicate that Marlowe became a successful playwright, not so much
by the merit of his university education but through the experience
he gained as a professional student of the theater.

The Authorship of *Tamburlaine*

In the eighteenth century, Malone had assigned the authorship of
Tamburlaine to Nashe. Although the 1826 Pickering edition of Marlowe's works begins with parts 1 and 2 of *Tamburlaine*, the editor holds
that Heywood's prologue to *The Jew of Malta*, where the evidence of
Marlowe's authorship was purportedly contained, does not prove that
Marlowe wrote *Tamburlaine*. It is necessary that Heywood's prologue
be furnished here in order to clarify the Pickering editor's point.

> We know not how our play may pass this stage,
> But by the best of poets in that age,
> The Malta Jew had being and was made;
> And he then by the best of actors play'd:
> In Hero and Leander, one did gain
> A lasting memory: in Tamburlaine,
> This Jew, with others many: th' other wan
> The attribute of peerless, being a man
> Whom we may rank with (doing no one wrong)
> Proteus for shapes and Roscius for a tongue.[28]

These lines are not only bad as verse but they are also obscure as
evidence. The Pickering editor held that, while one is led to believe
that it was Marlowe who gained a "lasting memory" (line 6) by writing
"Hero and Leander" and *Tamburlaine*, it is possible that the way in
which "made" (line 3) is rhymed with "play'd" (line 4) may indicate
that Heywood was simply stating that Marlowe "made" the Jew and
that Edward Allen the actor "play'd" Tamburlaine. In his separate
prefatory remarks to the play, the Pickering editor finally concluded

that *Tamburlaine* "cannot be laid to Marlowe's charge."[29] In the particular edition that contains James Broughton's notes, one notices that Broughton, too, agreed with the Pickering editor. In longhand he notes that the "style [of *Tamburlaine*] is very similar to that of Peele's David & Bethsabe. The same expressions of the same ideas may be found in both plays."[30] In 1826, therefore, the consensus had shifted toward a cautious rejection of Marlowe's authorship of *Tamburlaine*.

Yet, in 1831, Collier claims to have "found" proof that Marlowe did in fact write *Tamburlaine*. In *The History of English Dramatic Poetry*, he announces an entry in Philip Henslowe's diary that had "escaped the eye of Malone."

Pd. to Thomas Dekker, the 20th of Desember, 1597, for adycyons to Fosstus twentye shellinges, and fyve shellinges more for a prolog to Marloes Tamburlan: so in all I saye payde twentye fyve shellinges.[31]

Thus Collier provided the first piece of substantial evidence for Marlowe's authorship of the play. This evidence has since been proven a forgery.

The question remains as to why Collier would commit such a forgery. It is certain that although there was other evidence that pointed toward Marlowe's authorship of the play, Collier could find no substantial or conclusive proof of Marlowe's authorship. Moreover Broughton, the prior authority, in his effort to relieve Marlowe of his bad reputation, argued on fairly solid grounds that *Tamburlaine* could not be ascribed to Marlowe with any degree of certainty.

There is little doubt, however, that both the Pickering editor and Broughton, both of whom were trying to vindicate Marlowe, saw the bombastic poetical language of *Tamburlaine* as a possible impediment to the new view of Marlowe they wished to establish. Collier's statements were made, however, after Broughton had asserted convincingly that Marlowe was treated unfairly by literary historians and had supplied him the fresh laurels of a misunderstood poet-martyr. (It is certain that Collier in *The History of English Dramatic Poetry* read Broughton's comments in *The Gentleman's Magazine* because he mentions the record of Marlowe's burial on the register at St. Nicholas Church; however, he fails to give credit to Broughton for finding it.) Arguably, after Marlowe's reputation had been defended by literary worthies, it could be said that the freebooting text of *Tamburlaine* was

[handwritten margin note: 1831 ✗]

[handwritten note at bottom: ✗ This spelling of the playwright's name must have come from The newe Metamorphoses, where Tamburlain is mentioned. Marloz was really Marlor, the r mistaken for z]

a literary experiment by a young genius. Collier was more concerned, after all, with constructing a larger framework for dramatic poetry than with contesting specific accounts of Marlowe's life. In fact by proving Marlowe's authorship of *Tamburlaine,* he actually strengthened his own argument.

Collier was the first outright apologist for a play in which even the most generous critics had found few worthwhile features. As early as 1820 he defended *Tamburlaine* against its detractors by saying that the hero's boasting is not "half so exaggerated and wind-swollen" as in such characters as Dryden's Almanzor in *The Conquest of Grenada* or as "ridiculous" as the speeches of Cethegus in Jonson's *Catiline.* His view remains the same over ten years later when he says that the "turgid" and "bombastic" language of *Tamburlaine* is pardonable because Marlowe is experimenting with a new and innovative verse form.

> Until it [blank verse] appeared, plays upon the public stages were written, sometimes in prose, but most commonly in rhyme; and the object of Marlow was to substitute blank-verse. His genius was daring and original: he felt that the prose was heavy and unattractive, and rhyme unnatural and wearisome; and he determined to make a bold effort, to the success of which we know not how much to attribute of the after excellence of even Shakespeare himself.[32]

Therefore by 1831, Collier, who convincingly dated *Tamburlaine* in the late 1580s, argued that the play offered the first use of blank verse on a public stage. Of course the use of blank verse in a play that also relied on popular stage spectacles for its dramatic effects predated the same kind of phenomenon in early (and arguably later) Shakespearean productions. Moreover, because the play's date coincided with other evidence that indicated Marlowe's presence in London, Collier could argue that *Tamburlaine* was a flawed first play by a young Marlowe that was followed by other pieces that are "in various gradations of improvement" (*The Massacre at Paris* excepted).[33]

What Collier achieved by one small forgery, therefore, was immense. By ascribing *Tamburlaine* to Marlowe, he gave a young author a rough first production and therefore supported his own view that Marlowe's work improved by varying degrees up to the advent of Shakespearean drama. Moreover, by contextualizing the history of blank verse, Collier made Marlowe the originator of the form on the popular stage. (He apparently missed some earlier uses of the form on

stage.) As an innovator of blank verse, a form that enjoyed a celebrated revival in the early nineteenth century, Marlowe became more
praiseworthy in the minds of those who cherished Milton and Wordsworth. Most important, Collier tied the study of the playwright firmly
to Shakespearean studies. Therefore, this one forgery gave Marlowe
an enormous boost in the canon of Renaissance dramatists. The
enduring strength of Collier's paradigm is evidenced by the fact that it
is roughly the same model scholars use to this day when tracing the
development of English drama.

Marlowe the Player

Dramatic productions, even successful ones, were not held in high
literary esteem during Collier's day. The low opinions held toward the
stage were accompanied by the equally low social status of actors in
nineteenth-century society. While some actors, such as Kemble, Sid-
dons, and Kean, seemed to enjoy much public popularity, the theater
itself was notorious for its attraction to the dregs of society both on the
stage and in the audience. Before Collier, critics of dramatic poetry as
a rule did not concern themselves as much with the actual acting or
stage production of various plays as they did with understanding the
quality of the poetry. However, not only did Collier describe particular elements of stage production in his *History of English Dramatic
Poetry*, but, by considering annals of the stage (vol. 1) and the actual
Elizabethan theaters and their appurtenances, he maintained that a
playwright must be aware of the function of the public stage in order
to write effective verse. He specifically wished to establish Marlowe
as a common player who rose to be an erudite poet.

This effort can be seen in another of his forgeries. After "proving"
that Marlowe wrote *Tamburlaine* and that the play brought blank verse
to the public stage for the first time, Collier goes on to examine
Marlowe's corpus in terms of his artistic accomplishments. Beginning
with *Tamburlaine,* Collier challenges the existing opinions about Marlowe; that is, he claims that the author of this learned poetry was in
fact an actor.

In order to confirm this biographical feature, Collier presented a
manuscript of a ballad called "The Atheist's Tragedie," which he said

referred to Marlowe under the anagram of "Wormall." The section of the ballad that is noteworthy here is as follows:

> A poet was he [Marlowe] of repute
>   And wrote full many a playe
> Now strutting in a silken sute
>   Then begging by the way
> He had also a player beene
>   Upon the curtaine stage
> But brake his leg in one lewd scene
>   When in his earlie age[34]

This piece of biographical "evidence" was repeatedly published throughout the century by the next three editors of Marlowe's works (Dyce, Bullen, and Cunningham).

It may have been that Collier was attempting to assert that the fine blank verse he surveys in *The History of English Dramatic Poetry* was written by a man from humble beginnings who had experienced both fortune and poverty (the "silken sute" and the "begging by the way"), and who had to resort to a lower profession for income in his youth. This of course would fit in nicely with the evidence that proved that Marlowe was a shoemaker's son. The above lyrical resume also seems to indicate that Marlowe's dramatic achievements were enhanced by unsteady fortunes and stage experience. This view would parallel Collier's own experience, since as a young man he had associated with the stage as a reviewer in order to supplement his father's sparse income. Ultimately, it seems that Collier forged "The Atheist's Tragedy" in order to use Marlowe as a historical example of the fact that fine dramatic writing requires a grass-roots understanding of the actual workings of the stage. Moreover, he probably came to this conclusion because he himself had begun his literary career at the center of the London theater district.

Some Final Speculations about Collier's Forgeries

The concept that native ability and effort overcome low birth would have been attractive to Collier. His rise from being the son of a hack to becoming one of the foremost members of the London literary society of his day is evidence of his extraordinary drive. It also suggests a strong desire for social advancement that was not only expressed in his literary efforts but in his early attempt to become a poet. In fact, he wrote an epic entitled *The Poet's Pilgrimage*, which was a pretentious effort to rediscover the Spenserian tradition.[35] Collier even goes so far as to employ the Spenserian stanza through some extremely clumsy passages in which a poet who is searching for Fame personified encounters a Pilgrim who advises him to abandon the quest, because Fame is fickle. This attempt to rework an anachronistic theme was doomed to fail. Yet it provides some insight as to why Collier may have been initially attracted to Marlowe and specifically to the playwright's story of the rise of Tamburlaine, who elevates himself by means of a powerful poetic meter.

As noted previously, Collier also noticed the resemblance between Spenser and Marlowe, finding passages that indicate strongly the former's influence on the playwright, as in the following lines in which Tamburlaine reflects on how the populations of conquered nations will receive him.

> To note me Emperor of the three-fold world;
> Like to an almond tree ymounted high
> Upon the lofty and celestial mount
> Of ever green Selinis, quaintly decked
> With bloome more white than Hericina's brows,
> Whose tender blossoms tremble every one,
> At every little breath that thorough heaven is blown[36]

Collier quotes these powerful lines ostensibly to call attention to Marlowe's use of the alexandrine in the last line here in and in other places in the play. This examination of Marlowe's craft leads him also to scan, almost obsessively, a section of *Edward II*. His long and short marks over Marlowe's lines not only show just how closely the bibliophile was reading Marlowe's dramatic poetry, but they also mark a peculiar personal intrusion into the "history" he is putting forward. It seems that Collier was willing to suspend history for a moment in order to search for the precise craft of Marlowe's stunning verse.

The close attention Collier gave to Marlowe's poetic form indicates that he saw a definite science in verse composition. If he did see the ability to write fine poetry as something that could be learned or acquired, then his philosophy would have been unique in a time when literary critics usually saw poetic capability as bestowed at birth rather than developed through an understanding of the craft. At any rate, Collier saw in Marlowe's poetry a development through *Tamburlaine* to *Edward II*, which means of course that Marlowe acquired poetic skill through practice. Moreover, specifically of Marlowe's hero, he says that "Marlow could not have selected for his purpose a better subject than the life and conquests of Tamburlaine, who rose from the lowest grade of life to the loftiest honours of a throne."[37] Again the idea of achievement and upward mobility is honored by Collier in a period when critics had little good to say about *Tamburlaine*.

His deep involvement with Marlowe's poetic craft indicates that Collier may have been trying to enhance his own poetic abilities by attempting to learn Marlowe's methods. This seems especially true when one considers another of Collier's forgeries that concerned Marlowe. The following doggerel rhyme demonstrates how Collier's interests in Marlowe's work were in fact obsessive. Collier "found" the lyric on the title page of a play called *An Alarum for London*, which he assigned to Marlowe.

> Our famous Marlow had in thys a hand
> As from his fellowes I do understand
> The printed copie doth his muse much wrong
> But natheless manie lines ar good and strong
> Of paris massaker such was his fate
> A perfitt coppie came to hand to late.[38]

According to Bakeless, this forgery fooled virtually no one. And no good reason has been offered since to suggest that the play was written by Marlowe. Bakeless also maintains that Collier even wrote his own name, "J. Payne Collier," on the title page and later inked over it to make it read "S. Leighe Collier."[39] This particular effort to misrepresent the authorship of a little-known play, when there seemed to be no advantage in doing so (unless he was simply trying to increase the size of Marlowe's corpus), provides an insight into the psychology behind Collier's forgeries.

One must keep in mind that Collier spent long private hours pouring over records to which he had exclusive access—records that in some cases had been left untended for many years. Without attempting psychoanalysis, it may be enough to say that Collier came to see these manuscripts as his own private possessions to do with as he pleased. Although these forgeries are clear enough now, the person who committed them may not have seen a clear distinction between the creation (or forging) of a history and the marking and misrepresentation of certain ignored documents.

His signature on the above title page, therefore, may have been a private act, which gives away something about the nature not just of Collier's reasoning but of the type of historical reconstruction that he was attempting to do. We have seen how he forged Henslowe's diary in order to strengthen his own theory of the history of English poetry. We have further seen how he adjusted Marlowe's biography into some vague resemblance of his own. His lyric above, which is accompanied by his signature, may be the overt representation of what Collier, as a historian, was implicitly doing all along. In effect, he manipulated Marlowe for his own purposes, an effort that was not distinct from actually re-creating the playwright in his own image.

The "Effective History" of Collier's Scholarship

It was not until Collier's announcement of the Perkins folio that suspicion began to mount over his scholarly credibility. Soon a number of scholars, many of them already chagrined over Collier's numerous discoveries prior to the folio, began to unravel the mystery of this seemingly oracular find. Although a heated debate continued throughout the decade, no one was allowed a close enough look at the folio to establish its authenticity. Collier, probably in fearful anticipation of what eventually resulted, gave the book to Devonshire, his patron, who cloistered it from any perusal that might prove inimical to Collier's reputation. The duke died in 1858, whereupon Frederic Madden, then a curator in the British Museum, prevailed upon Devonshire's heir to have the document examined. Under the meticulous eye, not of a Collier detractor, but of a British Museum staff member by the name of Hamilton, the Perkins folio was exposed for what it was. In the years to follow, Collier's life work would be thoroughly condemend as forgery upon forgery was uncovered.

It would seem that current scholarship, after years of exacting research, would have overcome Collier's unfortunate influence, but his Marlowe forgeries were repeated by critics for many years until they were checked. For instance, the forgery in Henslowe's diary that Collier used to establish Marlowe's authorship of *Tamburlaine* was not called into question until C. M. Ingleby's article in 1868. Among other authorities in this century, Bakeless in 1942 again confirms this forgery, noting that Collier's own edition of Henslowe's diary "makes no comment whatsoever on this entry." The forged ballad that Collier used as proof that Marlowe was an actor was exposed in the 1870s but not brought under scrutiny by an editor of Marlowe's works until Bullen's 1885 edition and not before several historical accounts of Marlowe had been written on the assumption that he was an actor. These forgeries and speculations, often recycled well into the twentieth century, can still perplex current researchers.[40]

Perhaps the most notorious example of a Collier discovery that still confounds researchers is the "Collier leaf," which is currently at the Folger Library. The leaf is a short excerpt of a scene from *The Massacre at Paris*, which, if genuine, would be the only surviving manuscript of any length written in Marlowe's hand. The first recorded reference to this fragment is in the prefatory note to *The Jew of Malta* in Collier's edition of Dodsley (1825). Collier states that it had recently been acquired by Thomas Rodd before he prints his transcription of the short excerpt in its entirety. The leaf is transcribed again several years later in *The History of English Dramatic Poetry* where Collier states that the holograph was in his possession. As Tannenbaum notes, however, the second transcription does not agree with the first.[41] The excerpt, which had never appeared prior to Collier's initial notice and transcription, passed into the hands of James Halliwell-Phillips and then probably from him to the Warwick Castle library. From there it came into the possession of Marsden J. Perry of Rhode Island, and eventually it was acquired by the Folger Library. In their work *In Search of Christopher Marlowe*, Wraight and Stern compare magnifications of what was believed to be Marlowe's signature on the will of a Mistress Katherine Benchkin to matching letters (M, a, r etc.) on the leaf. They further magnify one of Collier's forgeries to show the dissimilarities between Collier's "Elizabethan" hand and the handwriting on the leaf. Their evidence shows some similarity between the signature and the writing on the leaf.[42] Similarly, the recent *Index of English Literary Manuscripts* contends that there is equally no substantial reason to suppose the fragment a Collier forgery.[43] However, keeping in mind the nature of many of Collier's other discoveries, one is hesitant to draw conclusions about the validity of the leaf, especially because it fits the pattern of his other assertions about Marlowe.

For instance, Collier's forgery, if that is what it is, would have had a specific motive in the need to validate his paradigm of Marlowe's aesthetic development. Collier dated the *Massacre* between *Faustus*, which he felt was written after *Tamburlaine*, and *The Jew of Malta*, which he thought was Marlowe's fourth play. Collier argued that each play demonstrated an increased skill on Marlowe's part. While this argument may not hold up today, it was then a perfectly reasonable one with the exception of the *Massacre*, which, in Collier's own words, had "no pretensions to dramatic interest." Collier does note, though, that the play, in some parts, was "vigorously penned." If he could find evidence to demonstrate that the play was printed from poor transcriptions, then he could argue (as he did) that "much was omitted" from the *Massacre* and that "the rest was garbled," thus suggesting that the play was originally much better than its fragmented printed copy suggests. This he could do by falsifying a poor transcription himself and making sure that it differed from the printed copy of the play, both of which are features of the leaf.[44]

The way in which Collier uses this fragment, therefore, suggests that the play's artistic deficiencies were the result of poor penmanship instead of bad taste. Indeed, Collier notices how four lines of the manuscript are "at least as good as any other part of the play," an observation that leads one to believe that what is missing is perhaps more excellent verse. Finally, by presenting this manuscript, Collier also managed to add another fine but incomplete play to Marlowe's corpus. If Collier did indeed forge this leaf, then he left one of the most disturbing problems in Marlowe studies today.

Alexander Dyce and J. P. Collier

The curious relationship between Alexander Dyce and Collier was one that began with the congenial exchange of information but eventually degenerated as a result of professional jealousy. Dyce, whom Collier helped to provide the first reliable edition of Marlowe's works, was perhaps the only other person in London during the second quarter of the nineteenth century who was as knowledgeable of Renaissance drama as Collier. Nearly ten years younger than Collier,

Dyce had everything that his senior lacked. He held a degree from Oxford, and he enjoyed a secure income from his family's estate. Although there is evidence that Dyce was very capable of "pulling rank" on Collier, it seems that they started on reasonably congenial terms. According to Ganzel,

> They were close associates: together they had founded the Shakespeare Society and co-operated in publishing its tracts. For over a decade they had given one another continuous editorial assistance, their correspondence was full of bibliographical questions asked and answered, and each had publicly acknowledged his debt to the other.[45]

In the beginning, it seems that Dyce, because he lacked the elder's experience in literary research and editing, gratefully accepted whatever information Collier was willing to share.

As Collier's fame grew, however, Dyce's attitude toward him became more arrogant, and their relationship became more strained. There is every indication that it was Dyce, either because he was suspicious of Collier's work early on or because he was merely jealous, who took the initiative in what became their eventual breach. Dyce's reservations about Collier's work began after the success of Collier's *History of English Dramatic Poetry*. After receiving a copy of the well-received first edition from Collier, he responded that it probably would not sell because it was dull and inelegant.[46] Thirteen years later Dyce spent what must have been months preparing an acerbic attack on the 1844 Collier and Knight edition of Shakespeare.

> Had I committed to paper all the remarks which occurred to me during a careful perusal of Mr. Collier's and Mr. Knight's editions of Shakespeare, they would have far exceeded the limits of *a single volume*. . . . but the Publisher very reasonably disliking a bulky book, it became necessary to make the present selection, and consequently to weaken the force of my protest against those two editions.[47]

Dyce supplies a thorough three-hundred-page list of "errors" in the edition. Judging from the amount of detail (and indeed the harsh tone of some of his observations), Dyce's "remarks" were an attempt to discredit not only the edition but Collier himself.

While Dyce may have been at times inspired by professional jealousy, there is no doubt that he shared with Collier an unrelenting drive to provide the answers to numerous questions that still permeated the field of Renaissance drama. His skillful research and his editorial thoroughness are at their finest in his 1850 edition of Marlowe's *Works*.[48] He combed forgotten registers and histories with an unprecedented precision, beginning by inspecting the parish register of Saint George the Martyr in Canterbury to establish Marlowe's birthdate, and then uncovering for the first time certain details concerning his schooling, which were obtained from Haste's *History of Kent,* the Cambridge Matriculation-Book, and the Cambridge Grace Book.

Reading the preface to Dyce's edition, one is immediately aware of his skills both as a biographer and as a researcher. His work provided many accurate and essential facts concerning Marlowe's life, yet he also unknowingly propagated two key biographical errors. First, he repeated Broughton's account that Marlowe had been slain by Francis Archer, and second he held, on the basis of forged evidence, that Marlowe had indeed been an actor. The first came about as the result of an honest mistake (which would not be found until Hotson), but the second could have been detected by Dyce had he been alert enough.

Basically, what happened is that Collier, as part of several concessions he made to Dyce, drew the latter's attention to several key documents concerning Marlowe's life that referred, among other things, to Marlowe's career as an actor. Although Dyce gives credit to Collier for his pioneering research on Marlowe, he seems more than willing to expose any of Collier's possible shortcomings. In fact, at one point in his introduction, Dyce seems to go out of his way to chide Collier for overlooking the disparity between the two editions of *Dr. Faustus*.

> The earliest edition [of *Faustus*] yet discovered is the quarto of 1604; which never having been examined either by Marlowe's editors or (what is more remarkable) by the excellent historian of the stage, Mr. Collier, they all remained ignorant how very materially it differs from the later editions.[49]

Dyce's patronizing comment here echoes the tone of his review of the Collier and Knight edition of Shakespeare.[50]

Dyce let the spirit of bibliographical one-upmanship divert him from what could have been an early exposure of Collier's methods. While he was looking for gaps in Collier's research, he failed to realize that certain documents that he had in his possession, such as Henslowe's diary, had been blatantly forged. We know from Dyce's preface that Collier had an interest in editing Marlowe's plays but abandoned the project after learning that Dyce had begun work on an edition himself. Dyce also refers to some "curious documents" kindly provided to him by Collier that the latter had planned to use in his own edition. While Dyce obviously accepted this assistance as per-haps yet another effort by Collier to win his goodwill and friendship (which it seems Collier did at several points), he did not seem wary at all of Collier's professional reliability. In fact, it seems more correct to say that he haughtily accepted Collier's help and then forthrightly bit the hand that fed him. Dyce searched the nooks and crannies of records to find Collier's omissions or mistakes, but he failed to look under his nose at the actual documents Collier gave him. The results were disastrous.

While our knowledge of Collier's bibliographical habits imme-diately leads us to suspect foul play, Dyce not only innocently re-peated Collier's Marlowe forgeries, but he went to great lengths to accommodate his own research to Collier's "findings." At the end of Dyce's preface, for instance, is a familiar lyric that Dyce says that Collier "found" on a title page of a copy of *Alarum for London*. This was the same title page on which Collier blatantly signed, and then struck out, his own name. Collier, it seems, was prepared to use this forgery in his own edition of Marlowe's *Works* to prove that Marlowe was the author of *Alarum for London*. When it turned out that Dyce was to do the edition, however, Collier forwarded it to him. Although Dyce prints the lyric, he does not challenge the suggestion it contains that Marlowe wrote the play. Underneath the lyric, Dyce concludes that the "report of Marlowe's 'fellows' may be true: but certainly in the *Alarum for London* (as we now possess it) no traces of his genius are discoverable."[51]

Dyce was thoroughly fooled, however, by the "The Atheist's Trag-edie," which was almost certainly written by Collier himself. He even includes the ballad, in its entirety, in volume 3 of the *Works*. In his introduction, Dyce refers to a manuscript copy of the ballad that was in the possession of none other than Collier, and he cites it as additional proof that Marlowe's father was a shoemaker. Later Dyce uses the same ballad to reassert the fact that Marlowe was an actor.[52]

Although he accepts the authenticity of this lyric without question, Dyce has some trouble with the fact that it indicates that Marlowe was first an actor and then a dramatist. This assertion would, of course, call up some questions as to how Marlowe managed his extensive schooling and a career in acting before the mid-1580s, when it was thought that he wrote *Tamburlaine*. To this problem, Dyce responds that

> the words of the ballad, "When in his early age," [do not] necessarily confirm the statement of Phillips [that Marlowe rose from actor to drama-tist]. In the stanza just cited, the ballad-monger (who found "age" an obvious rhyme to "stage") meant, I conceive, no more than this,—that Marlowe's histrionic feats took place soon after he had formed a perma-nent connection with the London theatre, for the sake of a livelihood; and, as far as I can judge, such really was the case.[53]

Here Dyce struggles to match evidence forged by Collier with his own discoveries of Marlowe's record at Cambridge instead of calling Collier's research into question. What is ironic is that both Marlowe's rise as an actor and (up to that time) his authorship of *Tamburlaine* (which puts him in London as a young man) were both established on the authority of Collier's forgeries.

Dyce's reliance on a contrivance like "The Atheist's Tragedy" compromises his serious and thorough effort to establish certain facts concerning the life of Marlowe. As mentioned above, Dyce uses the ballad to back up other evidence that indicated that Marlowe's father was a shoemaker and to confirm that Marlowe himself was an actor. Further into his introduction, Dyce discusses Marlowe's reception during the sixteenth century by vindicating, on moral grounds, Mar-lowe's life-style. While this matter will be explained in full below, Dyce's use of "The Atheist's Tragedy" here provides another ironic inaccuracy. Dyce footnotes his remarks concerning the poverty in which Marlowe and those in his company must have lived by saying that the "author of 'The Atheist's Tragedie' has not failed to notice such vicissitudes of fortune in Marlowe's case."[54] Then Dyce quotes a passage that indicates that Marlowe had mixed fortunes. Dyce was correct in saying that the "author" did not fail to notice the "vicissitudes" of Marlowe's fortune, but this author was probably a nineteenth-century bibliophile, and the "Marlowe" of the lyric was a product of fantasy, not fact.

It may be going a little far to say that Collier was intentionally duping Dyce by offering him false information concerning Marlowe. Collier, of course, after claiming to have found this information, would not have wished to draw any suspicion to his work by holding it back. It is certain, however, that Collier had reason enough to wish Dyce ill fortune in the latter's literary career. Dyce's treatment of Collier both privately and professionally became more and more arrogant as Collier's reputation grew as an editor and as a historian. While the two shared professional interests and even managed to work together at times, by the 1850s it was certain that Dyce had grown overly jealous of Collier's success. (Several years later, when Collier's forgeries of the Perkins folio were exposed, Dyce would become one of his most ardent accusers.) In the light of Dyce's earlier attacks on Collier, both in his reviews and even in his introduction to Marlowe's *Works*, it seems as if Collier obtained a kind of revenge on Dyce no matter what Collier's original intentions actually were.

Dyce's Marlowe

Unlike Collier, Dyce focused on Marlowe's university training. However, he shared with his associate the propensity for projecting features of his own life onto the life of the playwright. Dyce's account of Marlowe's life viewed the playwright as a young Cambridge scholar who should have received holy orders, but who instead went to London and took up stage acting and playwriting, and Dyce, who himself had turned from the ministry to enjoy a secular literary career in London, found some parallels between his and Marlowe's life.[55] Indeed, he treats Marlowe's alleged atheism and his life-style in a manner unlike any prior biographer.

It is plain that Marlowe was educated with a view to one of the learned professions. Most probably he was intended for the Church; nor is it unlikely that, having begun even during his academic course, to entertain those sceptical opinions for which he was afterwards so notorious, he abandoned all thoughts of taking orders. . . . Eventually he joined the crowd of adventurers in the metropolis with a determination to rely on his genius alone for a subsistence.[56]

What one also notices here is the Reverend Dr. Dyce's Christian tolerance for what he saw as a young man's decision to turn away from the ministry and pursue a more artistic and secular career.

Dyce is willing unapologetically to give Marlowe credit for *Tamburlaine*, a judgment that is made clear by one of the more memorable passages of his introduction.

> With very little discrimination of character, with much extravagance of incident, with no pathos where pathos was to be expected, and with a profusion of inflated language, *Tamburlaine* is nevertheless a very impressive drama, and undoubtedly superior to all the English tragedies which precede it.[57]

As with Marlowe's life, Dyce does not fail to defend a play that had been approached cautiously by most critics before him. He is also forgiving of Marlowe's "shortcomings" as a dramatist when considering such thematic problems as the buffoonery in *Faustus* or the "overcharged" speeches of Barabas in *The Jew of Malta*.[58]

Dyce's account of Marlowe's life and of the society into which he fell also recalls more the environs of the nineteenth- than the sixteenth-century theater. Using Henslowe's description of Tamburlaine's clothing, Dyce asserts that

> the Scythian conqueror, gorgeous in his 'copperlace coat and crimson velet breeches' [Henslowe], riding in a chariot drawn by harnessed monarchs, and threatening destruction to the very powers of heaven, was for many years a highly attractive personage to the play-goers of the metropolis.[59]

Dyce's picture of "highly attractive" characters seen by "playgoers" in a "metropolis" calls to mind the atmosphere of the nineteenth-century stage more than it does any arena, public or private, of the 1580s and 1590s.

As for the reports of Marlowe's degeneracy, Dyce defends the playwright by pointing out more about the social "milieu" of the theater district. However, Dyce describes the environs of the theater during his times, not Marlowe's.

Though the demand for theatrical novelties was then incessant, plays were scarcely recognized as literature, and the dramatists were regarded as men who held a rather low rank in society: the authors of pieces which had delighted thousands were generally looked down upon by the grave substantial citizens, and seldom presumed to approach the mansions of the aristocracy but as clients in humble attendance on the bounty of their patrons.[60]

Again, while this observation may hold true for the late sixteenth century, the allusions to the low social rank of dramatists seems more applicable to the social status of many who were affiliated with the nineteenth-century stage. Although many sixteenth-century playwrights did not fair well financially, there were those who did, and there were also many, like Marlowe, who were considered "gentlemen" by virtue of their university educations regardless of their financial status.

Dyce's remarks on Marlowe, therefore, provide a critical interpretation limited to the editor's understanding of the theater and the social status of playwrights during his own time. Dyce further states that, "[u]nfortunately, the discredit which attached to dramatic writing as an occupation was greatly increased by the habits of those who pursued it: a few excepted, they (the playwrights) were improvident, unprincipled, and dissolute,—now rioting in taverns and 'ordinaries' on the profits of a successful play, and now lurking in the haunts of poverty till the completion of another drama had enabled them to resume their revels."[61] Therefore, in his defense of Marlowe, Dyce nonetheless distances himself from the playwright by making a class distinction. If one understands that unruly behavior is common to the lower classes, then one may understand how an inspired playwright like Marlowe behaved as he did. He simply fell in with a bad crowd.

Keeping in mind Dyce's background, then, one can begin to see how he is able to praise, without fear of reproach, a shoemaker's son from a position of moral certitude and social stability. Finally, he states that at "a somewhat later period, indeed, a decided improvement appears to have taken place in the morals of our dramatic writers: and it is by no means improbable that the high respectability of character which was maintained by Shakespeare and Jonson may have operated very beneficially, in the way of example, on the playwrights around them."[62] Thus the Elizbethan playwright is intro-

duced to the Victorian age. The "better" playwrights are here assessed to exhibit higher moral fiber, and had Marlowe been fortunate
enough to have been born a few years later, he would no doubt have
benefited morally through the influence of his artistic superiors. Although one is to assume that Marlowe's downfall came about through
his imprudent contact with the lower classes, his work can still be
considered highly, since it was written by a scholar and artist who was
not fortunate enough to benefit from the moral influences of the
golden age of English drama.

Through the type of patronage that Dyce offers Marlowe here and
in other places during his introduction, he was able to praise the
playwright's works perhaps with more confidence than any critic
before him. Dyce saw Marlowe as immoral, but as such this could
only constitute a shameful reminder of human frailty. It seems safe to
say that Dyce, assuming the socially and morally superior role that he
did, was able to praise Marlowe's work without having either his own
critical judgment or his moral rectitude called into question.

Influences on Later Work

Unfortunately, the inaccuracies of Dyce's work would remain authoritative for the following thirty-five years, a period that saw the
voluminous production of literary histories and student manuals. Seldom did the writers of these histories read Dyce's work closely
enough to suspect Collier's foul play. Yet when later critics did find
discrepancies in earlier research, they usually used them as a license
to say anything they wished about the playwright.

Collier's exposure, too, went through a delayed reaction in the
literary community. Although his work drew suspicion during the late
1850s, the 1870 Cunningham edition of Marlowe's *Works* repeated the
forged information found in Dyce's edition. Cunningham, who held
the rank of lieutenant-colonel, in fact managed to create a new
Marlowe myth by claiming that the playwright must have "trailed a
pike" or "managed a charger" in the Low Countries because his
"familiarity with military terms and his fondness for using them are
most remarkable."[63] (Cunningham also suggests that Marlowe probably gained his propensity for using oaths during this time in the
military.)

In 1885, A. H. Bullen, taking into account Collier's bad habits, manages to distill the creditable scholarship from all the prior forgeries and misconceptions and so returned the matter of Marlowe's stage career to the more suitable region of the unknown.[64] By Bullen's time, though, literary research had already been professionalized to the point of specialization. Editors, researchers, critics, and historians, while they all shared common ground, failed to reach a consensus on certain crucial points concerning Marlowe's life and work. For the most part, commentators on Marlowe drew upon the information that they needed to prove larger points without checking or qualifying their references. Moreover, the bulk of material that concerned Marlowe in one way or another was reaching huge proportions with the advent of literary studies and with the help of additional research and criticism from the Continent. The result was that Marlowe became a completely misunderstood literary figure.

By the second half of the nineteenth century, Marlowe scholarship managed to remove the playwright from the damning consensus of rumor into a kind of intriguing enigma. The speculations over his life and death and the thought-provoking themes of his drama were features that began to interest critics in the playwright for all of the wrong reasons. Victorian moralists and the new breed of romantic idealists, both of whom embellished solid research with imaginative speculations, created various schemes for the interpretation of Marlowe's works. The result was that Marlowe's status rose even higher, and by the turn of the twentieth century, he would be considered by most second only to Shakespeare in the field of Renaissance dramatic poetry.

3

The Institutionalization of Marlowe

MARLOWE was fashioned into a romantic not during the early nineteenth century but well after the English romantic period.[1] The scholarship of Broughton, Collier, and Dyce in the first half of the nineteenth century was used, in the second half, not to temper the conjectures of earlier centuries, but to produce an even more sensationalized and extravagant portrait of Marlowe than before. Most Victorian critics ignored the fact that these researchers had called into question specific reports about Marlowe's lewd love affair, his blasphemous remarks, and his violent death.

Critics were more than willing, however, to credit any new evidence that would further contribute to the mythical image of Marlowe that they seemed determined to retain. For example, although Broughton's discovery that Marlowe was buried near the reported scene of his final knife-fight became general knowledge, his able defense of the playwright's character had little lasting effect on later biographies. Also, the evidence from Collier's forged ballad (which suggested that Marlowe was an infidel who broke his leg during a lewd histrionic feat) made its way into almost all considerations of Marlowe's character, whereas the understanding of Marlowe as a self-made poet did not. Similarly, the puritanical sixteenth-century condemnations of Marlowe's life-style, which were reproduced by Dyce, were often repeated as verifiable assessments of Marlowe's character although Dyce had strongly questioned their validity. Aside from the three researchers discussed in the previous chapter, few critics seemed even remotely concerned with separating facts from conjectures until Bullen clarified the record in 1885.[2]

Marlowe's biography was sensationalized during the mid- to latter nineteenth century, however, not so much because Victorian critics were being purposely disingenuous, but because they were becoming more and more obsessed with supporting current political, social, and educational concerns in their critical interpretations of old literature. The period, marked by the birth of many different ideologies and philosophies of history and literary studies, was overrun specifically by two diametrically opposed forms of thought: the first was fueled by a movement among educators to moralize English literature and to make it accessible to a mass reading public, while the second was provided by those among the literati who were purposely antagonistic to the political and social values of Victorian society.

Victorian views of Marlowe therefore can be grouped under each of these two categories. In this chapter, the first will be examined in order to show how information about Marlowe was gradually distilled so that the playwright could be moralized and included in the study of English literature. In their efforts to provide a canon of writers who were fit for students and interested middle-class readers, Victorian educators came to regard Marlowe as a type of early, high-minded romantic. Ironically, the playwright's reported excesses became a necessary by-product of his spiritual search for beauty and truth. Because *Faustus* also seemed to reaffirm traditional moral beliefs, it became more popular and well-received even though most pre-Victorian critics had found little value in the play.

Marlowe among the Masses

A fundamental change occurred in the nature of literary criticism during the nineteenth century that was rooted in a movement to popularize English literature and to introduce literary studies first into working-class schools and later into the universities. Roughly speaking, at the beginning of the century, Renaissance studies were part of the limited domain of the erudite and leisured class. The critics of this period were more journalists, editors, poets, or connoisseurs who found in the Renaissance an innovative poetic spirit that many of them wished to regenerate in their own time. Moreover, their literary commentaries usually reached only a select group of readers.

During the mid- to late nineteenth century, however, critics sought to elevate the study of English and to establish literary study in schools and universities because of its "civilizing" effect on the middle and working classes. As Terry Eagleton and Chris Baldick have recently argued, the new proponents of literary study, taking

into account Matthew Arnold's view that a general understanding of
culture placates certain less-refined social instincts (such as dissent
and revolt), were socially conscious educators instead of antiquarians
or connoisseurs. They also saw English literature as "a popular sub-
stitute for the classics," and soon there were basic English requirements at training colleges and a perfunctory understanding of English
was required by public examination boards.[3] Influenced by this new
"social mission" of English pedagogy, educators took up the study
and teaching of literary texts with more energy than ever before, and
eventually a form of literary knowledge was disseminated (albeit
thinly) among the middle and working classes.[4]

Because these efforts did in fact improve the status of English
studies, the process of canonization began to take on a new significance. More and more new as well as reprinted old books were being
mass-produced, but it was impossible for one to read all of the works
that were considered valuable. The educator had to choose the most
"important" texts for study not just for a limited group of interested
readers but for the many students of literature. This was an age-old
problem in the humanities, but it was intensified when the educator
took on the social responsibility of insuring that a large number of
students received the proper exposure to the great works in a limited
amount of time. Furthermore, because the curriculum was open to an
endless variety of literary texts, certain priorities had to be established, many of which ring familiar today. Does a work exhibit the
representative features of its "era"? Does it fit into a chronological
line of artistic ascent and descent? Does it present conflicts and
situations that are common to all? And, most importantly, does it
somehow reaffirm desirable social and moral beliefs?

As early as the 1830s, Henry Brougham, Charles Knight, and other
publishers began a movement to provide "useful knowledge" for
public, and specifically lower-class, edification.[5] William and Robert
Chambers also contributed profitably to this cause in a variety of ways,
but in none so significant as their *Cyclopaedia of English Literature*
(1843–44), which enjoyed immediate popularity and was reprinted
often throughout the century.[6] The Chambers history had the ver-
satile quality of providing either self-help for the student or servicable
information for the literary novice.

The itinerary of the *Cyclopaedia* was quite different from those of
prior histories, which were more assemblages of biographical scraps

and critical evaluations for private consideration than they were guidebooks or instructional tools for society in general. On one hand, the *Biographia Dramatica* (1812) was popular among scholars, critics, and reviewers, but it did not have the scope of a literary history. On the other, the encyclopedia works sponsored by Lardner (1831–51) and Hallam (1839), while they thoroughly covered English literary history, were far broader in scope than the more focused entries of the *Cyclopaedia*.[7]

There are several features of the *Cyclopaedia*'s entry on Marlowe that foreshadow trends in future histories. Chambers basically reports the knowledge of the day concerning the playwright: that he was a shoemaker's son, that he received an M.A. from Cambridge, that he suffered an untimely death. The entry also exhibits its debt to Collier's research by ascribing *Tamburlaine* to Marlowe and quoting the forged ballad that indicated that Marlowe was a bawdy actor. Because Collier's habits were not then known, the ballad was still fair game, yet the entry continues by embellishing both Meres's and Wood's contention that Marlowe was killed in a duel with a rival although the account had been previously discredited by Broughton.

> Marlowe had raised his poniard against his antagonist—whom Meres and Anthony Wood describe as 'a serving-man, a rival of his lewd love'—when the other seized him by the wrist, and turned the dagger, so that it entered Marlowe's own head. . . .[8]

Although the entry reports recent biographical discoveries, it maintains the Meres and Wood accounts without fully establishing the fact, as Broughton had done, that both biographers were themselves reporting hearsay.

Like Lamb, Chambers also presents excerpts from Marlowe's plays. These excerpts, though, are not presented to expose the reader to fine poetry but to demonstrate the "characteristic features" of Marlowe's "high-sounding" blank verse.[9] The entry provides, moreover, a biographical sketch and much more critical commentary than the *Specimens*. In fact, the *Cyclopaedia* attempts to organize Marlowe within a concise framework of pre-Shakespearean drama.

> The greatest of Shakespeare's precursors in the drama was Christopher Marlowe—a fiery imaginative spirit, who first imparted consistent

character and energy to the stage, in connection with a high-sounding and varied blank verse.[10]

One immediately notices that this entry was not written to provide critical explanations, glosses, or additional information for someone who has already read Marlowe's plays. Instead, by including "characteristic" passages from each of Marlowe's major works, it provides just the kind of biographical, critical, and textual information one would need to signal a familiarity with the playwright that one did not really have. Although Gross states that the guide was "primarily intended to be read for pleasure" he suggests also that students "may have found it handy for reference purposes."[11] Therefore, Chambers's guide could have been used sufficiently for test "cramming" or covering gaps in one's reading.

Chambers's entry on Marlowe had these features because it was obliged to report information concerning the playwright to an essentially naive readership. Because Marlowe had a limited amount of space, the entry could report only those elements which suited the perceived "era" within which he wrote. It was generally accepted that pre-Shakespearean playwrights were well-educated but given to excess and unrefined stylistic experimentation. However, nothing is mentioned of the enormous disagreements between scholars over major features of Marlowe's life and works. The entry, therefore, focuses on characteristics of the playwright that suited a predetermined historical pattern; however, the skepticism among scholars concerning the validity of certain early biographical reports was apparently not considered "useful" knowledge for public consumption. Therefore Chambers, by reporting certain details and not qualifying others, was actually drawing a line between two types of knowledge: the useful and authoritative knowledge provided to the masses, and the skeptical knowledge of informed scholars. Through a type of administrative process that filtered out scholarly skepticism, Chambers provided a sensational image of Marlowe as an unruly pre-Shakespearean who was part of the general ascent of English drama.

The Chambers *Cyclopaedia* was not specifically a textbook, so there are limits to what one can deduce from it concerning how Marlowe may have been presented in the classroom. In William Spalding's *The History of English Literature* (1855), however, there is at least a superficial glimpse of how the playwright was presented to teachers during the mid-century.[12] Based originally on his lectures to Scottish teen-aged university students, Spalding's work, to use his words, was intended to be an "Elementary Text-Book to those who are interested in the instruction of young persons." It was specifically a teacher's manual that attempted to cover only the most important concerns of English study, from Caedmon's song onward.

In this survey, Marlowe is only a small addition to the age of Spenser, Shakespeare, Bacon, and Milton. The playwright is briefly described as the writer of "stately Tragedies, serious and solemn in purpose, energetic and often extravagant in passion, with occasional touches of deep pathos, and in language richly and even pompously imaginative."[13] Although almost nothing is said of Marlowe's biography, the mere description of his work provides a picture of an author who, although given to excess, had an essentially austere creative mission.

Spalding's overview of Marlowe and the pre-Shakespeareans was different from Chambers's because his survey was written for teachers and was considered more literary than biographical. Moreover, he found the chief literary concern of Marlowe's period to be that of religious reform. Marlowe, therefore, was necessarily united to his greater contemporaries by his own reformist characteristics (which Spalding obviously saw as few).

Yet, the more one marks the differences between these historical figures, the more they become resistant to this type of intellectual grouping. Ultimately, the provision of a more comprehensive historical understanding of certain writers makes it more difficult to "teach" them within well-defined notions of their era. Therefore the provision of "useful" classroom knowledge, in Spalding's history, allows for the omission of historical and biographical details, especially for minor figures such as Marlowe. While this is justified by the intellectual format (and the limited amount of space), the reader is provided nonetheless with a distinct impression of Marlowe as a reformer.

Spalding's perfunctory overview of Marlowe suggests much about the playwright's character that a more thorough examination of his life and work would not support. However, because Marlowe's contributions to English literary history are so confidently stated, Spalding's readers would have little reason to suspect that his general observation was not both creditable and commonly accepted.

Surveys such as Chambers's and Spalding's had a seminal influence

on the literary histories that became pouplar during the 1860s, somewhat concurrent with the growth of required English studies in
schools and universities. However, instead of merely reviewing Marlowe's verse, histories from the mid-century onward began to sub-
divide the playwright's features within highly exclusionary concepts
of English literary history. Often Marlowe's portrayal would only
provide a prop for larger ideas that were embodied by such catch
phrases as "the rise of drama" or "the spirit of reform." No two
historians followed exactly the same pattern; thus each rendition of
Marlowe had certain distinct and emphatic biases concerning the
nature of his life and works. These reports were ultimately more
damaging than the unsubstantiated accounts from earlier encyclope-
dias because they were read by far more people who were far more
likely to accept the authority of the printed word. Also during this
period, many more primers were printed that introduced the reader to
the theoretical classifications of literary schools, periods, and eras.
According to Gross, most of the literary histories of the 1860s were
"textbooks plain and simple." He further notes that "these books
were symbols of the homage which bureaucracy had been induced to
pay virtue. They [the histories] were partly designed for use in
colleges and schools, but even more for the benefit of candidates
hoping to pass Civil Service, I.C.S. and other public or professional
examinations, most of which included an English paper."[14] Perhaps
the most significant feature of these surveys, however, is that their
entries were shaped by a social need to present literary figures to
students in a morally redeeming manner.

For instance, in *A Complete Manual of English Literature* (1867),
produced by Thomas Shaw, the entry on Marlowe carelessly confirms
the tenuous biographical details (which were becoming by then somewhat of a tradition) while adding other assertions.[15] Again, there are
hints of Collier's "bawdy actor" ballad almost ten years after Collier
had been exposed. Again, the entry verifies certain biographical
accounts that had been discredited.

> His [Marlowe's] mode of life was remarkable for vice and debauchery,
> even in a profession so little scrupulous; and he was strongly suspected by
> his contemporaries of having been little better than an Atheist. His career
> was as short as it was disgraceful: he was stabbed in the head with his own
> dagger, which he had drawn in a disreputable scuffle with a disreputable
> antagonist, in a disreputable place. . . .[16]

While one does not expect a survey such as Shaw's to demonstrate the same biographical thoroughness as, say, the preface to an edition of Marlowe's works, one is surprised to find as much discrepancy between Shaw's account in the mid-1860s and Dyce's 1850 preface. Shaw's candor on the matters of Marlowe's disgraceful and disreputable career is simply unwarranted considering the then well-known tenuity of the supporting evidence.

It is obvious that, as an educator, Shaw was inclined to "disapprove" of Marlowe's allegedly flawed character. Yet, as an educator, he was charged to review the playwright's contributions because they were included in previous histories. Because these prior histories never established grounds for biographical accuracy, however, Shaw was free to say almost anything he wished about Marlowe. Shaw's condescending remarks were dated, though, as moral condemnations of Marlowe's life were beginning to become obsolete by this time. The general instinct to pronounce judgment on old literature, though, was something that he nonetheless shared with other historians during his time.

For instance, another of the histories that were published, like Shaw's, for pedagogical purposes was *A First Sketch of English Literature* (1873), an enormously popular work by Henry Morley.[17] Although more accurate than Shaw on Marlowe's biography, Morley goes to another extreme by simply leaving out all accounts of the playwright's life after Cambridge while using most of the entry to cover the eternal moral value of *Faustus*. Having no other exposure to Marlowe's biography, one would think that the author of this play was completely erudite and pious. Speaking of *Faustus*, Morley notes that Marlowe was responding to the spread of Continental religious reform in England by translating the German "Faust-book" "in his nobler way, taking the plot of his play either from the German original, or from this first translation, perhaps while it was yet in hand."[18] This and the fact that no mention is made of the possible causes of Marlowe's early death makes him out to be the noble moralist who, by writing *Faustus*, carried forth the torch of reform.

In these four mid-Victorian literary handbooks, one is provided with four entirely different Marlowes. Like Chambers, Shaw includes the sensational reports of Marlowe's death but uses them to condemn the playwright, whereas Chambers reports them as characteristic of the times in which Marlowe lived. Like Spalding, Morley presents Marlowe as a moral reformer but takes a specific interest in Marlowe's education, whereas Spalding does not. Thus Marlowe is characterized in these four histories as a passionate man of his time who was a stately and austere reformist, but who was nonetheless a disreputable rogue who had a taste for the obscene. The only feature that these views of Marlowe share is their tendency to provide moral overlays for their subject.

It would seem that what these interpretations lacked in originality they should have made up in biographical accuracy, yet this was far from the case. As demonstrated above, Marlowe scholarship became more conjectural and inaccurate by the 1860s than ever before. One could ignore this as being the result of quick research displayed in a limited historical format, but there are more profound reasons for this phenomenon. By the 1870s Marlowe, like all other ranking literary figures, had been subdivided and inducted into a number of histories that, because of their social and pedagogical significance, required a sound and socially acceptable understanding of the movements and developments within English literary history. Yet, this "knowledge," specifically of Marlowe, was provided exclusive of certain biblio-graphical facts.[19]

The notion of social education gave writers a strong desire to provide constant moral and cultural affirmation in the works and biographies they considered. Marlowe, because of his reputation, might have been lost in this movement had it not been for the critical appreciation he had gained earlier in the century. Also, because Shakespeare was by this time hailed as one of the most prominent antecedents of Victorian cultural achievement, Marlowe's well-estab-lished influence on Shakespeare also could not be overlooked. Not only did Marlowe's biography provide social and political scandals, however, but his plays also focused almost exclusively on the dark side of human nature. *Tamburlaine*, *Edward II*, and *The Jew of Malta*, plays that depict the worst kinds of human behavior, were hardly schoolboy or even middle-class material. The only work that could even remotely be read to reaffirm Victorian morality was one that had received very little appreciation before the advent of English studies.

The Rise of *Faustus*

The histories by Chambers, Spalding, Shaw, and Morley are also interesting because of what they had to say about Marlowe's *Faustus*.

Chambers gives priority to the play in his entry on Marlowe (quoting at length from the scene of Faustus's damnation); Spalding calls it "one of the finest poems in our language"; Shaw asserts that "Marlowe's best work is incontestably the drama of *Faustus*"; and Morley uses most of his entry to discuss the drama.[20]

Before the mid-nineteenth-century advent of instructive histories of English literature, though, there was no strong appreciation for the play. After a popular but brief run on the sixteenth-century stage, the play virtually disappeared from record, and by the eighteenth century the story had degenerated to a puppet show. In 1744, Dodsley's first choice was *Edward II*, and Reed, in 1780, added not *Faustus* but *The Jew of Malta*. In 1781, Warton saw *Faustus* as a display of silly superstitions. Lamb did not have much to say about the play in 1808, and neither did the editor of the 1826 Pickering edition.

Faustus did receive some guarded praise for some of its speeches in the early nineteenth century, but it seems that these remarks were made only because Marlowe's popularity in general was increasing. In fact, both Hazlitt and Broughton asserted that *Edward II* was Marlowe's best play. Collier, in the chronological hierarchy he presented for Marlowe's artistic assent, would have found *Faustus* at least third on the list and perhaps even lower. Therefore the play seems to have been appreciated yet not revered as Marlowe's finest play until well after the 1830s.

By the middle to the latter part of the nineteenth century, though, many critics found *Faustus* to be the epitome of Marlowe's dramatic achievements. Chambers and Spalding, in the 1840s and 1850s, and later Shaw and Morley, in the 1860s and 1870s, were not alone in their enthusiasm for the play. Cunningham, in his 1870 edition of Marlowe's *Works*, called *Faustus* Marlowe's greatest play, and Bullen, while he felt that much of the play was not penned by Marlowe, said in 1885 that it was "a work which once read can never be forgotten."[21] Generally speaking, most critics of Marlowe in the second half of the nineteenth century treated the play with more regard than before.[22]

There are several possible reasons for the increasing critical status that *Faustus* began to receive during the nineteenth century. Editors and scholars were attracted to the play because of the disparity that Dyce had pointed out between the 1604 and 1616 quartos. Moreover, the German legend of Faustus intrigued commentators both in England and on the Continent. In the years following Dyce, two separate editions were printed, both with elaborate introductions covering

the growth of the Faust-legend and giving editorial suggestions as to
how the extensive textual differences between the two quartos should
be resolved.[23] Textual uncertainty, however, usually damages the
reception of a literary work, so it may be drawing a false conclusion to
say that the play's growing popularity rested on the concerns of a
handful of textual scholars.

There is also no doubt that Goethe's profound influence on English
letters led to a closer look at Marlowe's work, yet this seemed to have
a contradictory effect on its reception. Marlowe's plot was considered
by some to be one of the possible sources of *Faust,* yet Marlowe's
artistry was overshadowed by what many thought to be one of the
greatest poetic achievements of all time.[24] Lovers of Goethe and
German philosophy often considered themselves travelers of the
higher road of Continental letters and were careful not to voice too
great an appreciation for the dubious achievements of one of Shakespeare's contemporaries. Some were even standoffish when it came to
non-Shakespearean Renaissance drama. G. H. Lewes, for instance, in
his influential and well-received discussion of the life and works of
Goethe, says *Faustus* has "many magnificent passages, such as Marlowe of the 'mighty line' could not fail to write; but on the whole it is
wearisome, vulgar, and ill-conceived."[25]

It seems that the growing appreciation for *Faustus* was rooted in
another phenomenon, which had to do with the advent of English
education. The study of English required a comprehensive curriculum that could be covered in a limited amount of time by a greater
number of people from a wider variety of social and cultural back-
grounds. Chambers was the first "historian" who published a literary
guide for these purposes, and he was one of the first to give priority to
the consideration of *Faustus.* The other surveys that lauded the play
did so, it seems, because they were written by educators for roughly
the same ends as Chambers sought: the review of useful (and required) knowledge. Spalding was a professor of logic, rhetoric, and
metaphysics at the University of Saint Andrews. Morley was a professor of English at University College, London, and Shaw held a
position at the University of St. Petersburg, Russia, and then became
professor of English to the grand dukes.

Faustus, therefore, was first held in higher esteem by educators who
saw that the study of literature should have a certain amount of
redeeming social value.[26] Although Marlowe's works provided abun-

dant examples of immorality, *Faustus* had a theological model that at least ostensibly reaffirmed the traditional presuppositions of Christian moral judgment. It is easy to see how the educator might be drawn chiefly to the discussion of this rather than another play by Marlowe. The play historically had mass appeal. It had survived in certain carnivalesque adaptations throughout the seventeenth and eighteenth centuries, and its theme of damnation was accessible. Finally, it could be taught in schools without taking on the politically and socially disturbing issues (such as anti-Semitism and homosexuality) that are prominent in Marlowe's other plays.

By the early 1870s, it is apparent that educators had provided grounds to introduce a moral Marlowe to the university. There was also a contrary hint that the playwright was being fashioned into a passionate romantic in the mold of Shelley and Byron. Yet the image of Marlowe as a romantic would not be thoroughly refined until a romantic literary theory itself was provided by later educators. Once romanticism became a discipline for the reading of old texts, many educators would begin to see Marlowe as second only to Shakespere in dramatic accomplishment during the Renaissance.

Institutionalized Romanticism

The continual problem Marlowe posed for educators in the second half of the nineteenth century was rooted in how they should interpret the playwright in a morally redeeming manner. He had been established as a historically significant figure by able scholars and as a worthy poet by reputable critics. He therefore had to be included in all thorough discussions of the Renaissance. Yet, no matter how his biography was adjusted or how the themes of his works were framed, Marlowe's contribution to literary history could not be praised too highly simply because the example of his life and the themes of his works were largely unfit for students.

In 1870, though, Edward Dowden, then professor of English literature at Trinity College, Dublin, made an observation that indicated that a new attitude toward Marlowe was surfacing.

[It is] amongst the pre-Shaksperians that we find the man who, of all the Elizabethan dramatists, stands next to Shakspeare in poetical stature, the one man who, if he had lived longer and accomplished the work which lay clear before him, might have stood even beside Shakspere, as supreme in a different province of dramatic art.[27]

Both the idea that Marlowe stood "next" to Shakespeare and the notion that had he lived his "art" would have developed in the way that Shakespeare's did in the years after 1593 were brave conclusions for an academic to reach in the 1870s. Yet Dowden was voicing what would become the opinion of many critics of the late nineteenth and twentieth centuries.

Marlowe's status rose to this lofty position as a direct result of a movement, strongly supported by Dowden himself, to employ the precepts of German romantic philosophy as a general theory for the interpretation of English literature. While the transcendentalism of German poetry and philosophy had been a popular subject for many years in England among the well read, it gathered a new momentum with the advent of English studies.[28] Educators began to group English poets by their general poetic sensibilities and discuss them in terms of a shared artistic consciousness. Specifically, the early nine-teenth-century English "Romantics" began to be viewed as a group of artists and philosophers whose higher aesthetic concerns provided the appropriate precepts for the study of literature. Their political and religious beliefs, however, were generally considered secondary to their artistic pursuits and therefore deemphasized. Moreover, examples of atheism, debauchery, and dissent, when they did arise, were seen not as outgrowths of the radical temperament of their time but as symptoms of the poet's individual artistic struggle.

The educator's search for transcendental values in English literature became therefore a highly moral project even if a particular poet were on record as being immoral. The excesses of Byron and the atheism of Shelley were often viewed as necessary passions in search for beauty and truth. Ironically, because immoral behavior was vital to the poet's agonistic quest for transcendence, it became tolerable. Even the most outlandish and depraved behavior was received as part of an essentially moral pattern.

The literature of the Elizabethan and Jacobean periods was also basically removed from its own history and consigned to the new ideology of high romantic philosophy. Specifically, educators began to interpret Renaissance literature as a forerunner of romanticism and

Marlowe, precisely because of his scandalous reputation, as being an early romantic himself. There is no better example of this type of textual interpretation than in Edward Dowden's literary criticism.

Dowden's Literary Theory

Before attempting a discussion of the critical treatment of Marlowe from the 1870s onward, Dowden's literary methodology should first be closely considered because his theoretical stance provides a fulcrum on which Marlowe scholarship turns to this day. Dowden's appraisal of Marlowe was higher than any critic before him, and it began a trend among educators toward dehistoricizing certain crucial features of Marlowe's life and works.

Born in Cork, Ireland, on 13 May 1843, Dowden was the son of a successful linen draper and had been reared as a Protestant. Apparently a gifted thinker, he took his degree from Trinity College, Dublin, where he was awarded unusual academic distinction.[29] Although his degree had prepared him in Divinity, he never took holy orders. Evidently drawn to the study of metaphysics, he eventually disavowed the Christian faith altogether. Dowden did not abandon the notion of spiritual transcendence, however, by rejecting the church. It seems more correct to say that a nonunified church did not facilitate his search for a genuine philosophical standpoint that was both affirming and aesthetically appealing. According to Ludwigson, Dowden acquired from German ontological models of unity, forwarded specifically by Hegel, Schelling, and Fichte, an affinity for the type of spirituality provided by transcendental thought. The tenets are as follows:

(1) the concept of the universe as "oneness"; (2) a dialectical resolution of the contradiction between freedom and necessity; (3) the moral imperatives involved in the union of the real and the ideal; (4) the imagination as the bond effecting the union between the real and the ideal, the sensory and the supersensory.[30]

On broader terms, Dowden believed that the conflict between the actual and the ideal could lead to universal oneness through transcendental contemplation. Moreover, he found that this type of philosophical intercourse was more spiritually rewarding than traditional religion.

In his critical approach to the Elizabethan era, therefore, Dowden sought to unite Renaissance literature with the verisimilitude of German philosophical idealism. For instance, the idea of conflict and resolution that Dowden forwards in his following comments from *Shakespeare: A Critical Study of his Mind and Art* (1892) places the playwright's life and work within a noticeably romantic dialectic.

> Shakspere lived and moved in two worlds—one limited, practical, positive; the other a world opening into two infinites, an infinite of thought, and an infinite of passion. He did not suppress either life to the advantage of the other; but he adjusted them, and by stern and persistent resolution held them in the necessary adjustment.[31]

Dowden's view not only of Shakespeare but of the Elizabethan age in general is shaped by his understanding of metaphysics—specifically of the quiddity of metaphysical unity both in nature and in human reason.

Looking more closely at Dowden's criticism, one notices also that he finds in Shakespeare a genuine or "real" culture, something both organic and concrete, which is antithetical to the abstract or ideal. He uses Cardinal Newman's treatise to clarify this approach to Shakespeare and the Renaissance in the opening of his discussion of Shakespeare. Dowden in fact quotes Newman's observation that, as historians, when we analzye the "real," we rise

> "from particulars to generals, that is, from images to notions. . . . Man is no longer what he really is, an individual presented to us by our senses. . . . He is attenuated into an aspect, or relegated to his place in classification. Thus his appellation is made to suggest, not the real being which he is in this or that specimen of himself but a definition."[32]

Dowden's course in his discussion of the Elizabethan period is to attempt a comprehension of Shakespeare and his "age," while understanding that such an attempt is necessarily muddled by his historical distance from his subject.

This said, though, he does hold that Elizabethan literature historically represents a natural or prephilosophical environment that in a sense provides a certain amount of objective data for the ideologically informed critic.

> There is perhaps no body of literature which has less of an expressed tendency for the intellect than the drama of the age of Elizabeth. It is the outcome of a rich and manifold life; it is full of a sense of enjoyment and overflowing with energy; but it is for the most part absolutely devoid of a conscious purpose. . . . Capacity for perceiving, for enjoying, and for reproducing facts, and facts of as great variety as possible,—this was the qualification of a dramatist in the days of Elizabeth. The facts were those of human passion, and human activity.[33]

The point here is that the interpreter's (Dowden's) purpose in reading cultural history is to provide this "conscious purpose" and in fact to graft an entire *post facto* set of cultural values onto the text. Dowden understands this "historical" or factual world of Elizabethan drama as being necessarily in conflict with the ideals of romantic philosophy. Yet through the "sensibility" of his interpretation, one that seeks a unifying principle, a resolution is reached. And, perhaps more accurately, through an interpretive exercise that conjoins the real and the ideal, the historical text or artifact becomes part of the "wholeness" of cultural history. Therefore, the lesson learned from a Renaissance text is not one of an actual or distinct historical nature but one that requires the understanding that Renaissance discourse is a fundamental part of an overall cultural design.

In fact, the "actual" is displaced to the act of interpretation, from which a pure experience may be derived. When the actual text conflicts with ideology, the interpreter or critic resolves or synthesizes the two opposing forces. The result, of course, is apotheosis.

> A vigorous, mundane vitality—this constituted the basis of the Elizabethan drama. Vigour reveals on the one hand the tragedy of life. Love and hatred, joy and sorrow, life and death being very real to a vigorous nature, tragedy becomes possible. To one who exists languidly from day to day, neither can the cross and passion of any human heart be intelligible, not the solemn intensities of joy, the glorious resurrection and ascension of a life and soul. The heart must be all alive and sensitive before the imagination can conceive, with swift assurance, and no hesitation or error, extremes of rapture and of pain.[34]

This critical passage indicates that the study of a pure cultural environment extracted from history can be used to heighten the reader's
awareness of an ultimate or transcendental truth. To do this, though,
he or she must assume a greater philosophical awareness than the text
does itself; in essence, the reader must gain a certain amount of
interpretive authority over the text.

Keeping in mind Dowden's rejection of the church, one is led to
think that he was substituting, quid pro quo, church for culture—
specifically a culture whose political and literary bodies he believed
were struggling for transcendence through unity. One may also assume that Dowden saw his efforts to interpret culture as an essentially
sacred project. Instead of affirming a religious faith that was in a sense
dead because its practice required more liturgical replication than
critical invention, he chose instead what he saw as the more vital and
sacrosanct role of cultural priest.

Dowden's reading of Shakespeare and of Renaissance literature,
therefore, was an exercise in affirming an erudite and informed sense
of cultural destiny. Because Dowden depoliticized the Renaissance
and (re)formed it to provide a base for romantic interpretations of
culture as a unified whole, his literary theory argued for the value of
"transcendental" learning not as a precedent for social change but as a
justification for political and social stasis. (It should be noted that
Dowden distanced himself from Irish "revolutionary" poets and cam-
paigned ardently for Irish and English political unity.) Therefore,
ultimately Dowden's philosophy allows the cultural critic to incorpo-
rate the subversive, degenerate, or "non ideal" into a metaphysical
conflict with the "ideal" and, though interpretation, reach order
through resolution.

Dowden's interpretive methodology also provided him with a metaphor for the proper maintenance of social order. Using this literary
theory, it could be said that the concrete and factual world of the labor
force requires the custodial and interpretive direction of the ideologically informed intelligensia in order to achieve political and social
wholeness. This would affirm the Arnoldian idea that the proper end
of cultural studies in schools and universities was one that should
contribute to the maintenance of social order. Through this type of
literary reckoning, Renaissance literature was finally groomed for
serious study in the late nineteenth-century universities.

The "Ideal" Marlowe

Dowden's interpretation of Shakespeare reflected the erudition of a learned educator but not the objectivity of a scholar. Not only did he discount much of the historical research available to him, but he essentially removed the study of Shakespeare from "history" as he considered the achievements of past authors in relation to certain abstract notions of transcendental truth. While his predecessors had voiced these same romantic views in their considerations of old literature, Dowden's overall understanding of the organic, and thus aesthetic, unity of the Renaissance provided the most vivid example of the intellectual forces that shaped Marlowe criticism in the university during the rest of the nineteenth century and arguably much further.

Dowden's interpretation of Marlowe was contained in his view that the Shakespearean period provided a "natural" foundation for his romantic overview of literary history. In an essay first published in the *Fortnightly Review* and later in his *Transcripts and Studies* (1888), Dowden argues that Marlowe and others were organically intertwined with the "family" of Shakespeare.

> The study of Shakspere and his contemporaries is the study of one family consisting of many members, all of whom have the same life-blood in their veins, all of whom are recognisable by accent and bearing, and acquired habits, and various unconscious self-revealments as kinsmen, while each possesses a character of his own, and traits of mind and manners and expression which distinguish him from the rest.

After evaluating Shakespeare's prominent contemporaries, Dowden then makes the startling observation that Shakespeare "would have been master of the realists or naturalists; Marlowe, master of the idealists."[35]

Through the magic of literary theory, Dowden here transforms Marlowe into a romantic idealist when, before, the playwright had been considered sporadically talented but unrefined. Through this brief critical statement, however, Dowden provides Marlowe a highly significant position in the study of Shakespeare. The playwright would also be given an important place in Dowden's general understanding of literary history. This matter, though, requires some explanation.

In the early part of the nineteenth century, critics began to see Renaissance drama and poetry as a preromantic burst of literary energy that gradually exhausted after the accession of James I. With the exception of Milton, English literature was viewed as falling into an overall decline during the Restoration and eighteenth century. The influence of German romanticism compelled Victorian critics to import Continental writers in order to fill in this historical gap. (Later, Eliot and other modernists rebuilt the canon in a similar manner by disregarding the romantics and emphasizing instead the contributions of the French symbolists). Because Dowden and his contemporaries informed literature with certain transcendental notions of a Continental instead of a purely national cultural assent, German philosphers and playwrights were often included in the English canon because of their influence on English letters of the early century. This, in a sense, completed the canon in a way that suggested that "European" thought was important but only as it contributed to the sensibility of English literature.

Dowden's description of Marlowe as an inspired dramatic idealist provided an illuminating comparison with Shakespeare. Moreover, Dowden forms in this comparison a dialectic that he related to the differences between Goethe and Schiller:

> Shakspere and Goethe are incomparably the larger and richer natures, their art is incomparably the greater and more fruitful; yet they were themselves much greater than their art. Shakspere rendered more by a measureless sum of a man's whole nature into poetry than Marlowe did; yet his own life ran on below the rendering of it into poetry, and was never wholly absorbed and lost therein.[36]

Also Marlowe, like Schiller, "seems to have lived in and for his art. His poetry was no episode in his life, but his very life itself."[37] Dowden here draws a distinction between the high canon of writers whose work was driven more by a real life force and the lower canon of accomplished but artificial idealists. Therefore Marlowe is used to "unify" the Renaissance poetic sensibilities with those of the German romantics by complementing Shakespeare's realism with his converse idealism. This holistic thinking removes Marlowe from his traditional historical position as a pioneering and influential pre-Shakespearean dramatist and elevates the playwright to a loftier place as an example of one of the essential components of the "eternal" poetic consciousness.

By romanticizing Marlowe in this way, Dowden is able to place the playwright's biography in an entirely different light than before. Because Marlowe's poetry was, according to Dowden, "his very life," he had to abandon the prospects provided by his university education, "return to the poverty from which he had sprung, and add to poverty the disgrace of an actor's and playwright's life."[38] By suggesting that Marlowe's impoverished and disgraceful life-style was essentially an outgrowth of his poetic quest for the ideal, Dowden ultimately maintains that Marlowe's immorality, like that of other romantics, was necessitated by his search for a higher state of being.

Another way in which Dowden elevates Marlowe's moral position is by explaining the playwright's reported excesses in the light of his intellectual struggle with the church. Although there was no evidence that supported this notion, Dowden weaves this conjecture into an ostensibly factual consideration of the playwright's biography. For instance, he accurately reports the assumed dates of Marlowe's plays, yet he takes interpretive liberties that make Collier's forgeries pale in comparison. Speaking of Marlowe, Dowden says that the playwright

> had behind him . . . terrible religious and political battles, and the downfall of a faith. For his [Marlowe's] own part, taking art as the object of his devotion, he thrust all religions somewhat fiercely aside, and professed an angry Atheism. The Catholic hierarchy and creed he seems to have hated with an energy profoundly different from the feeling of Shakspere, distinguished as that was by a discriminating justice.[39]

The disavowal of religion, the angry atheism, the hatred of Catholic hierarchy all contribute to create a believable but highly tenuous portrait of Marlowe's character based on the scant amount of biographical proof of his personal beliefs and attitudes. In fact, taking into account Dowden's Protestant upbringing, his participation in the Irish unionist movement, and his avowed atheism, his understanding of Marlowe's personality reflects more about his own experience with "religious and political battles," his own dislike of the Catholic hierarchy, and his own disenfranchisement with the church.

After Dowden, Marlowe's works enjoyed a status that they had never had before, and it seems as if this heightened appreciation for the playwright was made possible by a critical methodology that wove Marlowe into a complex romantic understanding of the literary canon. The result, to echo Dowden's quotation from Cardinal Newman, was that Marlowe was no longer who he was. Because his work had shortcomings, he was considered an idealist, and because his idealism was essentially moral, he was pardoned for his atheism and his immoral behavior. The great irony of this gesture of critical absolution was that much of Marlowe's bad reputation had been based on forgery and hearsay to begin with.

Because Dowden's literary theory established a romantic discipline for the study of the individual accomplishments of great men, it removed the consideration of Marlowe from loose artistic and moral judgments and instead contained him within the dialectics of German romantic philosophy. As a poet and idealist Marlowe was suspended above normal moral standards and held up as an early example of one who provided the most noteworthy features of the romantic consciousness.

Marlowe after Dowden

No matter how Marlowe was fashioned by historians in the latter portion of the nineteenth century, his atheism and his career as an actor continued to play an essential part in biographical considerations of his literary career. Dowden's reappraisal of Marlowe, however, provided the educator/historian from the 1870s until the end of the century with much more interpretive latitude. In short, in this self-consciously scientific age, the critic's intuitive judgment became as credible as historical facts.

Not all thinkers were convinced that romantic interpretations were acceptable, however. As part of the reaction to the obvious lack of objectivity in romantic views of history, a French positivist, Hippolyte Taine, in *A History of English Literature*,[40] surmised that history can be empirically reconstructed by an accurate consideration of three primordial and environmental forces: the race, the surroundings, and the epoch. He therefore took what seemed to be a more scientific approach to the study of history.

Although Taine's work was published before Dowden's observations, his English translation and impact came afterward. Also, the original work in French had been inspired more by a need to provide a deterministic history of English literature than to educate the masses. However, its translation (1873) by one of the masters at the Edinburgh Academy, H. Van Laun, was enormously popular in England during its time. While writing in the nonromantic spirit of environmental determinism, Taine's observations on Marlowe were nonetheless just as distorted by the historian's fidelity to timeless overarching ideas.

Speaking figuratively of the pre-Shakespearean era, Taine says that its genius "forced its way" amid "low places," "dunghills," excess, and violence from which Marlowe rose, the "true founder of the dramatic school." Although Taine documents this observation by citing historical examples, there are a few matters that he fails to clarify when discussing Marlowe specifically. Marlowe, he says, "was an ill-regulated, dissolute, outrageously vehement and audacious spirit, but grand and sombre, with the geniune poetic frenzy; pagan moreover, and rebellious in manners and creed." While one familiar with Marlowe's works has no trouble believing this, the remark is presented as being irreproachably true. Considering that Taine was using the same source material that others had questioned before him, his observation here is too confidently stated.[41]

Further along in his discussion, using quotation marks to feign that he is actually quoting Marlowe, Taine asserts that the playwright

> denies God and Christ, blasphemes the Trinity, declares Moses *"a juggler,"* Christ more worthy of death than Barabbas, says that *"yf he were to write a new religion, he wolde undertake both a more excellent and more admirable method."* [my italics]

Scholars of Marlowe would recognize instantly that the substance of the above account is taken from the Baines note, parts of which were provided in the appendix of Dyce's 1850 edition of Marlowe's complete works (Taine even footnotes this himself). Yet Dyce and others before him had clearly stated that this note comprised second-hand reports made by Baines concerning Marlowe's atheism. Taine, however, arranges this material to make it seem unquestionable that Marlowe actually said these things himself, concluding that "such were the rages, the rashnesses, the excesses which liberty of thought gave rise to in these new minds."[42]

Using more information from Dyce's preface, Taine draws a dazzling portrait of Marlowe's life after Cambridge by saying that "on his return to London, in want, amid the license of the green-room, the low houses and taverns, his head was in a ferment." Then Taine claims that Marlowe "turned actor; but having broken his leg in a scene of debauchery, he remained lame, and could no longer appear on the boards." He ends this description by repeating Wood's account of Marlowe's stabbing himself during a fight over a lewd woman.[43]

By employing a supposedly empirical methodology, Taine single-handedly did more damage here to the objective consideration of the life of Marlowe than any other nineteenth-century historiographer. Most likely Taine's single source was Dyce's 1850 preface, which repeats the known accounts of Marlowe's life but roughly within the context of the circumstances within which they were written. As Broughton had concluded years earlier and as Dyce had further noted, the reports of Baines, Vaughan, Wood, and others were unreliable, yet Taine repeats them with no qualifications. The result is that Dyce's conjectures become Taine's facts. This problem was also compounded by the restatement of information, drawn from the forged "Atheist's Tragedy," that Marlowe had broken his leg during a bawdy scene.

Taine's way of presenting Marlowe's life, while more than slightly disingenuous, is no doubt influenced by his need to show positivistically how Marlowe's degenerate life-style was "determined" by the corrupt environs in which he lived. Those who had suggested this before Taine (Dyce, for instance) did so in defense of the playwright's reputation. Taine, however, merely used accounts of Marlowe's life to validate his contention that the pre-Shakespearean period was marked by its corruption. Although not given to the ambiguities of Dowden's romanticism, Taine's review of Marlowe's life suggests that his historical methodology, despite its claims to empiricism, is driven by the same absolutist notions of era and Zeitgeist that plagued Dowden's work and other prior historical surveys.

In both Dowden and Taine, one can see how two theoretically different ideological stances, both using the same sources and both resolute on revealing the truth about literary history, provided two entirely different renditions of Marlowe's life. Moreover, both works were published for students and the English reading public by educators in the spirit of forwarding an accurate view of English literary history.[44]

It was, however, the Dowdenesque, or the romantic, view of Marlowe that persisted within academe and in literary history. Shortly after Taine, William Minto, yet another Scottish professor, issued a literary survey entitled *Characteristics of English Poets* (1874).[45] This work sought specifically to refute Taine's deterministic premises and returned to the Dowdenesque context that heralded individual achievement. Although in his preface Minto says that his method "is not so much the opposite as the complement of M. Taine's," Minto in fact rejects Taine's methodology completely.

> I might advance, as a justification of my attempt, that a thorough study of the individual is indispensable to that higher study which has for its object the determination of the characteristics of the race. And besides, the most interesting study for mankind will always be the individual man.[46]

As professor of English literature at Aberdeen, Minto demonstrates that unwillingness to forego the study of the individual which is strongest in the academic mind. Taine's cultural determinism made literary figures seem less heroic; it also undermined the notions of individual achievement touted in schools and universities.

Minto's understanding of Marlowe's life, however, was not as given to conjecture as either Dowden's or Taine's. For instance, Minto emphasizes that the reports of Marlowe's atheism were not conclusive.

> Marlowe's alleged writings against the Trinity have never been seen; in all probability, like some alleged infidel works of the Middle Ages, they never existed.

Yet, he departs from this type of scholarly skepticism by representing the playwright as a tempestuous artist.

> Beauty, which he [Marlowe] worshipped with passionate devotion, was the only sunshine of his life, and it shone with a burning fierceness proportioned to the violence of his tempestuous moods.[47]

Therefore, although Minto questions the reports of Marlowe's atheism, he provides the playwright with a fabricated personality.

Because a greater emphasis was being placed on Marlowe's romantic qualities, most historian/educators after Dowden generally reported fewer biographical details concerning the playwright's life and instead dwelt on the immortality of his dramatic achievements. Not only were considerations of Marlowe's life brief, but they usually offered highly inspired versions of his supposed romantic temperament. For instance, A. W. Ward, professor of English literature, Owens College, Manchester, echoes the sentiments of both Dowden and Minto when he covers Marlowe in his *History of English Dramatic Literature to the Death of Queen Anne* (1875).

> The element in which as a poet he [Marlowe] lived was passion; and it was he and no other who first inspired with true poetic passion the form of literature to which his chief efforts were consecrated. . . . it is this gift of passion which, together with his services to the outward form of the English drama, makes Marlowe worthy to be called not a predecessor, but the earliest in the immortal company, of our great dramatists.[48]

Not twenty years before Ward's statements, this evaluation may have been thought to be considerably overstated, yet Dowden's style of romantic reading had invested such prestige in Marlowe's fictional character that it was very common for critics of the past century to praise him in this manner.

After romantic critical theory won the university, the romantic Marlowe continued to be passed along from historian to historian, each with his own point to emphasize about the proper way to understand the playwright's life and works. After the 1870s, however, some of the rumors that surrounded the playwright's life were brought under control by able and competent scholarship. Most important, the authenticity of the forged "Atheist's Tragedy" was soundly challenged by C. M. Ingleby in a letter to *The Academy* on 1 April 1876. This eventually silenced the claim that Marlowe broke his leg during a lewd scene, and it weakened the argument for his atheism. Although the ballad was not a substantial piece of evidence to begin with, the information it carried had been crucial to almost every historical account of Marlowe's life for thirty-five years. Also, as is the case with misinformation, the bawdy tone of the ballad still sounded even after the evidence had been withdrawn.[49]

One of the final noteworthy histories in which it occurs is in T. H.

Ward's *The English Poets* (1880). A. C. Bradley, the young author of the entry on Marlowe, states that "an old ballad tells us that he [Marlowe] 'brake his leg in one rude (sic) scene, When in his early age.' " However, Bradley hints at having some knowledge of the ballad's questionable origins in his next sentence, where he states: "If there is any truth in the last statement, we may suppose that Marlowe gave up acting and confined himself to authorship."[50] This disclaimer, however, does little to discredit the ballad. All in all, Collier's forgery was not completely removed from the interpretive field of Marlowe's biography until Bullen, in 1885, resolutely contended that he had "little hesitation in pronouncing the ballad to be a forgery."[51] For a thirty-five-year period, during which authoritative literary histories were distributed among a wide reading public, the ballad was accepted as fact. It should be added that these histories remained popular for years and even decades after their initial publication, and later editors did not always revise certain false assumptions concerning Marlowe. (Fledgling students of literature who are in pursuit of catalogued information concerning literary history can readily find the works covered above in university libraries to this day.)

The uncovering of Collier seemed ultimately to have a positive effect on Marlowe scholarship, however, because after the 1880s critics began to be much more careful to qualify their observations of Marlowe with disclaimers much like the one Bradley used. The final decades of the nineteenth century was further a period that saw the advent of relentlessly meticulous Renaissance literary scholars: Furnival, Fleay, and, later, Greg, just to name a few. However, even the advent of the professional scholar did nothing to undo the romantic but moral Marlowe.

In 1880, A. C. Bradley provided a concise example of how Marlowe was generally treated by educators well into the twentieth century. His entry on Marlowe, like Ward's, placed less emphasis on the playwright's life and more on the historical value of his plays. Yet, he does give some specific consideration to Marlowe's character. "Marlowe," he says, "has one claim on our affection which everyone is ready to acknowledge; he died young." Bradley continues by grouping Marlowe with other romantic early deaths such as Chatterton, Burns, Byron, Shelley, and Keats. After speculating about the reports of his life, Bradley notes that the playwright, because of his youth, "lived in a free and reckless way." However, Bradley finds this recklessness the expected course of life for a young and impassioned poet. He concludes by stating that "whatever his [Marlowe's] offences may have been—and there is nothing to make us think he was a bad-hearted man—he had no time to make men forget them. He was not thirty when he met his death."[52] The pathos that Bradley evokes here had become a stock feature of Marlowe biographies by his time. This convention arose because Marlowe's pathetic life was paralleled to the tragic circumstances of the playwright's own heroes. Thus Marlowe became, by the end of the nineteenth century, thoroughly fictionalized as a type of dramatic hero.

Bradley's treatment of Marlowe demonstrates the virtuosity one would expect from the author of *Shakespearean Tragedy*. Of Marlowe's dramatic characters, he says, "they know nothing of half-heartedness or irresolution. A volcanic self-assertion, a complete absorption in some one desire, is their characteristic. That in creating such characters Marlowe was working in dark places, and that he developed them with all his energy, is certain,."[53] After admitting that Marlowe may have sought inspiration in "dark places," Bradley sharply contends with Hazlitt's remark that there was in Marlowe a "hunger and thirst after unrighteousness." He is careful to note that Hazlitt, by saying that Marlowe sought unrighteousness, did not mean that the playwright could not produce "true poetry." By drawing a line between the unrighteous mind and the true poetic vision, Bradley makes a key distinction—one that was of crucial importance to the Victorian educator. That is, although a great poet may do immoral things, his poetry must be understood as morally pure.

Bradley ends his consideration juxtaposing Marlowe with Shakespeare:

> it is only Shakespeare who can do everything; and Shakespeare did not die at twenty-nine. That Marlowe must have stood nearer to him than any other dramatic poet of that time, or perhaps of any later time, is probably the verdict of nearly all students of the drama.[54]

Although this statement is purposely inconclusive, one cannot help but think that Bradley is putting the finishing touches on the Marlowe who was gradually sculpted by a variety of critical efforts during the nineteenth century. Although literary historians were at first undecided as to which version of Marlowe to produce, the influence of romantic literary theory finally won out and Marlowe became yet another romantic. Furthermore, he was related more closely to Shakespeare and to later romantics through a perceived genealogy of poetic idealism. Through the work of Bradley (who lived until 1933) and others, the romantic and moral image of the playwright and his perceived importance in literary history has remained strong in the academy throughout the twentieth century.

4

Marlowe among the Aesthetes

In his biography of Hart Crane (1937), Philip Horton mentions that during Crane's years in New York the impassioned young poet once ran wildly down the streets of Little Italy shouting "I am Christopher Marlowe." Those familiar with Crane's work know that he read Marlowe and was influenced by his dramatic poetry. Crane, however, was no doubt attracted to other then infamous features of the playwright's life that mirrored some of his own excesses, specifically his wild drinking bouts and back-alley encounters with sailors near the docks of Hoboken. Horton even suggests that the poet felt himself "possessed by a Marlovian demon." In this chapter the origins of Crane's "demon" will be traced through a maze of critical stances taken by nineteenth-century literati who made a cult of Marlowe.[1]

It has already been demonstrated that Marlowe's life and works were moralized by Victorian historians and educators. For entirely different reasons, there were also other notable efforts made by the nineteenth-century literati to manipulate the playwright's image. Although these critical views departed from the status quo, many of the same forces that shaped the interpretation of Marlowe in academe also influenced the literati. Neither Dowden's romanticism nor Taine's empiricism was confined to purely pedagogical quarters. The critics covered in this chapter, however, used the playwright not to affirm but to contest the political and social conventions of their time.

Moreover, the audiences who were targeted by these critics were made up of a mixed bag of interested literary hobbyists, intellectuals, reformists, and whoever else wished to expose themselves to the extravagant and the avant-garde. While these interpretations of Marlowe may not have reached as many readers as did the educators' version of the playwright, they are still important in that they influenced the later views of many well-known writers such as Hart Crane. Ultimately, through the efforts of the literati, the understanding of

Marlowe's life and works plunged even further into the abyss of conjecture and imaginative speculation.

The Death of Christopher Marlowe

The first full-fledged literary attempt to assign Marlowe to a romantic canon came long before Dowden idealized the playwright. R. H. Horne, an associate of Leigh Hunt who shared Hunt's love of literature and his radical political opinions, wrote a one-act play entitled "The Death of Christopher Marlowe," which was printed in *The Monthly Repository* in 1837. The play was published later that year as a book, which was reviewed favorably in the same publication by Hunt himself. Because it is about the lives of Marlowe and other, at that time, little-known Renaissance dramatists, the play was obviously written for the intelligentsia. Although thematically tame by twentieth-century standards, it also broached sensitive social issues.[2]

Much like Broughton, Horne also sought to defend the playwright against moral condemnations from religious conservatives. Horne, however, purposely used and manipulated old unreliable reports because they made for a good story and, more significantly, because he wanted to use Marlowe's example to reaffirm the social need for the open expression of rebellious passions. Thus Horne's drama upheld the standard views that leftist thinkers took against what they saw to be an overly utilitarian and morally rigid society.

Horne's script provides a tale of a passionate actor/playwright who died in a tavern brawl over a lewd woman. He draws his story from two sources that had been soundly discredited by Broughton only a few years before: Wood and Beard, whom Wood footnoted (see Appendix A).

Horne adds several of his own touches to the story, also. Not only is Marlowe portrayed as a dramatic character, but Thomas Heywood and Thomas Middleton are also included in the cast. The play opens with a conversation between Marlowe and Heywood during which Heywood tries to dissuade Marlowe from pursuing further the love of one Mistress Cecilia. Marlowe, however, is too love-stricken to listen to reason. In response to Heywood, Marlowe says,

> Smile not; for 'tis most true: the very air
> With her sweet presence is impregnated richly.

As in a mead, that's fresh with youngest green,
Some fragrant shrub, some secret herb, exhales
Ambrosial odours; or in lonely bower,
Where one may find the musk plant, heliotrope,
Geranium, or grape hyacinth, confers
A ruling influence, charming present sense
And sure of memory; so, her person bears
A natural balm, obedient to the rays
Of heaven—or to her own, which glow within,
Distilling incense by their own sweet power.
The dew at sunrise on a ripened peach
Was never more delicious than her neck.
Such forms are Nature's favourites.

After this blank-verse confession, Heywood responds to Marlowe by reprimanding him for his imprudent obsession.

Come, come—
Pygmalion and Prometheus dwell within you![3]

Marlowe is portrayed as a compulsive but talented young poet whose obsessive love of a young woman, as Heywood notes, arises from the poet's own mutability and passion. The speeches of Horne's Marlowe, however, are conspicuously given to the celebrated theatrical styles and conventions not of the 1580s or 1590s but of Horne's own period. The lush imagery Horne's character uses makes the hero seem affected and mawkish. From the onset, therefore, Horne represents Marlowe as a nineteenth-century romantic, an unconsumptive Keats, whose excessive passions at once represent a pathetic but refined personality.

    After their opening conversation, Marlowe dismisses Heywood and his advice and proceeds to woo Cecilia, who happens onto the scene just after Marlowe reaffirms his amorous intents. Cecilia, who seems uninterested in Marlowe's urgings, indicates that she is no stranger to the company of men. She says to Marlowe,

Think'st thou I ne'er saw men in love before?
Unto the summer of beauty they are common
As grasshoppers.[4]

By the end of the first scene, the plot of a young romantic allured from reason by his infatuation with a common courtesan is apparent. The intensity of Marlowe's passions no doubt represents the curse of creative genius; that is, a poet may be so overcome by a vision of beauty that he is unable to see the apparent corruption of the object to which he is attracted. However, in order to apply this distinctly nineteenth-century aesthetic principle, Horne embellishes Wood's account of Marlowe's infatuation with a "certain woman" (see Appendix A).

Horne also defends the theater by adding to Wood's report certain sharp distinctions between inspired playwrights and common low-lifes who, although they are both of the theater district, are quite different in character. This distinction is drawn when Heywood and Middleton come upon the man whom Wood described as a "pimp." Horne names him Jacconot, and he, unlike Marlowe, is truly depraved. After a disgusted Middleton tells him that he will probably be hanged for his life-style (and his crude language), Jacconot retorts,

Well said, Master Middleton—May your days be as happy as they are sober and may your nights be full of applause! May no brawling mob pelt you when crowned, nor hoot down your plays when your soul's pinned like a cock-chafer on public opinion![5]

Although there is little doubt that audiences during the Renaissance were unruly, Jacconot's reference to the "brawling mob" and their hooting describes the early nineteenth-century theater. Therefore, Horne is suggesting that the playwrights, who are true artists and gentlemen, are required by the nature of their craft to mingle with the likes of Jacconot. He is also implying that Marlowe, like Heywood and Middleton, is a gentleman artist who, although he is found in the company of people such as Jacconot and Cecelia, is certainly not a degenerate.

Soon after his speech, Jacconot excuses himself from Middleton and Heywood so that he may rendezvous with none other than Cecilia. She is in debt to him for services of an unstated nature, but refuses to pay him back with her body, and Jacconot rebukes her for her hypocrisy. The second scene ends with Cecilia in soliloquy, expressing her desire to clear her conscience of her past deeds. This touch is entirely invented by Horne who wishes to show that although Cecilia is indeed corrupt, there seems to be something in her that

seeks reform, rather as in Dickens's Nancy (in *Oliver Twist*). Therefore, the reader is to understand that Marlowe, because of his sen-
sitivity and refinement, is able to see this feature in her character and
is seeking her out not for lustful gain but in order to save her from her
despicable life. When Marlowe's attraction to her is understood in this
light, he seems less the hellion that Wood had described. This whole
scenario of the fallen woman with inner idealism is, of course, more
the stuff of nineteenth-century melodrama or fiction than it is an
effort to reproduce accurately the life of a Renaissance dramatist.

The play ends after Jacconot enters and taunts Marlowe into a
jealous duel, during which Marlowe is stabbed with his own sword.
This sensational conclusion also includes an attempt to reject Beard's
(1597) puritanical indictment, which had stated that Marlowe died
while cursing blasphemously:

> (for hee even cursed and blasphemed to his last gaspe, and together with
> his breath an oath flew out of his mouth).

Horne no doubt found this account by checking Wood's reference to
it. Beard, however, did not even place Marlowe in a tavern but in
"London streets," and he gave Marlowe not a sword but a dagger.[6]

Although Horne includes a "cursing" speech, the oaths are directed to the murderer, not God, from the mouth of a desperate, not a
despicable, character.

> Bring life and time—bring heaven!—Oh, I am dying!—
> Some water—stay beside me—maddening death,
> By such a hand! O villain! from the grave
> I constantly will rise—to curse! curse! curse thee![7]

Not only does Horne omit Beard's contention that Marlowe was an
atheist, he indicates that the playwright was in fact religious by having
the hero invoke the image of heaven and the idea of rising from the
grave. Horne not only sentimentalizes the death of Marlowe, he uses
dramatic ambiguity in order to clear Marlowe of his bad reputation.
Generally, however, the play demonstrates how even the most worthy
characters can be unfairly condemned by the narrow-minded and
moralistic. Thus Horne achieves the same end as Broughton by using
an entirely different method—one that is consciously disingenuous.

This is even more evident in the last scene when a drunken

Marlowe responds to a gentleman's toast by waxing speculatively on the fickle nature of love, which he likens to the uncertainty of poetic immortality:

> Say, you do love a woman—do adore her—
> You may embalm the memory of her worth
> And chronicle her beauty to all time,
> In words whereat great Jove himself might flush,
> And feel Olympus tremble at his thoughts;
> Yet where is your security? Some clerk
> Wanting a foolscap, or some sportsman wadding
> To wrap a ball (which hits the poet's brain
> By merest accident) seizes your record,
> And to the wind thus scatters all your will,
> Or, rather, your will's object. Thus, our pride
> Swings like a planet by a single hair. . . .[8]

Marlowe's speech here is directed toward Wood and others who had previously condemned the playwright. However, it provides some irony because the speaker bemoans the vulnerability of historical records during a play in which the play itself represents a heavily revised image of a real literary figure.

Moreover, this same scene opens with a speech from a gentleman who predicts the immortality of Marlowe, Middleton, and Heywood—the three playwrights with whom he is drinking.

> I do rejoice to find myself among
> The choicest spirits of the age: health, sirs!
> I would commend your fame to future years,
> But that I know ere this ye must be old
> In the conviction, and that ye full oft
> With sure posterity have shaken hands
> Over the unstable bridge of present time.[9]

These lines mark an essential characteristic that distinguishes the motives of Horne and the literati in general from those of the educator/historian. Just as the nineteenth-century pedagogue reconstructed Marlowe for a Renaissance dramatic canon by assimilating history and philosophy, the nineteenth-century literati incorporated the playwright into an alternative canon by making no distinction between the author and a dramatic character.

Because Horne's play was printed in a journal that specifically sought to put forward radical political viewpoints, Marlowe's death, while it has a tragic outcome, still affirmed the inherent value of the free expression of human passions. Although the play does not seem particularly radical now, Leigh Hunt's review of "The Death of Marlowe" clearly indicates that Horne's play supported certain unconventional ideas when Hunt sentimentally recalls the Elizabethan past as a time when pure human passions could be expressed publicly.

> If the Old Globe, or Blackfriars Theatre, could suddenly be raised out of the ground, with those who just remembered the days of Marlowe for spectators, this were a piece to fill up an hour for them, to the content of those stout and truly refined souls;—souls that minced no matters in which humanity was discernible.

He then contrasts these "Elizabethan" passions with what he finds as the repressed moral restrictions of his own time by lamenting the fact that other tragedies were not as honest as Horne's.

> But who shall dare now-a-days to bring a courtezan on the stage, and find that she retains a heart in her bosom?

Therefore, according to Hunt, the play transgresses the boundaries of social propriety by providing a prostitute with a conscience.

Finally Hunt states the exact political point that was being made by Horne's reproduction of Marlowe's death.

> Extremes meet; and the new sense of a doubt of our moral perfection, falling upon a mechanical age, renders conventionality doubly sore and suspicious, and rebukes its want of courage and real innocence.[10]

The radical's hero, in Hunt's view, is the romantic whose disregard for the social norms of an industrialized society is "morally perfect" because it is essentially human and, above all things, natural. Horne's epigram to "The Death of Marlowe" is taken from Carlyle's recently published description of Mirabeau in *The French Revolution* and echoes this same sentiment. Marlowe, like the revolutionary, "was a man, fiery-real, from the great fire-bosom of Nature herself." Horne also dedicates his play to Leigh Hunt, a man whom Horne no doubt admired in the same light. In this dedication Horne distances himself from the proponents of "Useful Knowledge" and also expresses his contempt for Whiggish complaisance by saying that the play

> seems to deserve no such estimation as accrues to the very apparent labours attending the compilations of a Bridgewater Treatise (whereby our souls are elevated with the elaborately-proved resemblance of the Infinite to the finite) and other productions of the "Useful Knowledge" class: neither does it appear to claim the practical notice of a Whig Government, who are doubtless postponing their "good intentions" in order to let their old opponents, the Tories, walk over that "Dantesque pavement" and receive the compliments and thanks of all parties for the generous though tardy consideration of one [Hunt] who has so long worked for mankind.[11]

Although this statement is purposefully arcane, Horne makes it obvious that "The Death of Marlowe" is itself an attempt to assign the playwright not to a "useful" place in the development of English drama, but to a canon of romantics who, because of their unconventional life-style, were exemplars of political resistance. Ultimately, the play is important not because of its limited impact on Marlowe studies in the late 1830s, but because it was reprinted by Bullen later in the century when Marlowe was being included in another, even less politically direct canon.

Imagination and Fancy

Moving from Horne to Hunt, one finds another affirmation of Marlowe's poetic accomplishments that would fuel speculations by the literary avant-garde in the late-nineteenth century. Although one may be inclined to say that Hunt's criticism was "ahead of its time," it would be more accurate simply to point out that Hunt's radical observations on Marlowe influenced later critics who maintained them without all their politically subversive implications. Like Lamb and Hazlitt before him, Hunt, in *Imagination and Fancy* (1844), considers decontextualized excerpts from Marlowe's poetry in the light of their aesthetic quality. As he states in his answer to the question "What is Poetry?"

> Poetry, strictly and artistically so called, that is to say, considered not merely as poetic feeling, which is more or less shared by all the world, but

as the operation of that feeling, such as we see it in the poet's book, is the utterance of a passion for truth, beauty, and power, embodying and illustrating its conceptions by imagination and fancy, and modulating its language on the principle of variety in uniformity.[12]

This abstract view of poetry is perhaps difficult to accept as a tangible critical praxis, but Hunt's purpose in this work is actually less dreamy than it may seem at first. From the table of contents, one can see that he has a reformed historical viewpoint; that is, he groups Renaissance poets (Spenser, Marlowe, Shakespeare, Jonson, and Milton) with romantic poets (Coleridge, Shelley, and Keats) while conspicuously omitting the works of all writers between Milton and Coleridge.

Hunt's table of contents also demonstrates that he considers Marlowe to be more historically important than did the mid-century historians covered in the previous chapter. Marlowe, for instance, is considered independently after Spenser and before Shakespeare. The only other Renaissance poets who are discussed independently are Jonson and Milton. Even though Hunt's literary opinions are not as central as those of the more conservative historian/educator, his judgment influenced the literary community of his day. The fact that he holds Marlowe to be among the top ten English poets is startling considering that fewer than thirty years before the playwright was omitted even from critical discussions of "lesser-known" Renaissance dramatists such as Shirley and Brome.

Hunt's high assessment of Marlowe was rooted in the fact that he, like Horne, found the playwright to be a historical example of the romantic radical who shunned convention. Hunt does not remark on Marlowe's biography, perhaps because he is comfortable with the fictional image of the playwright that Horne had provided. There is something curious about some of Hunt's other omissions, however, which may furnish a clue as to precisely what he is trying to do with the playwright. For instance, Hunt never considers *Faustus*, *Edward II*, or the works that were possibly unfinished or collaborative efforts. Instead, he comments only on *Tamburlaine* and *The Jew of Malta*. Moreover, Hunt diverts attention from the features of those plays which detract from the political suitability of Marlowe's general example. Considering Hunt's role as a social reformer, it may be that he sees Marlowe's portrait of Tamburlaine and his parodic treatment of the Jew as furnishing examples of political violence and tasteless farce that were not acceptable to the radical camp.

While *Tamburlaine* fits the "romantic" pattern as an early example of overreaching (and blank verse), it supplies overabundant examples of power lust and violence. Untampered with critically the play's theme openly contests Hunt's view that the Elizabethan dramatic poets heralded an age of humanism, refinement, and sensibility. The expressions of political terror in *Tamburlaine*, therefore, are what he attempts to mute in his discussion of the play. He defends what he calls the play's "ranting" speeches by saying "besides the weighty and dignified, though monotonous tone of his versification in many places," the play has "passages in it of force and feeling."[13]

Hunt, therefore, focuses on the mechanics of the play instead of on its plot. The moments of violence are seen as being unimportant because they are expressed by a "monotonous" blank verse. Moreover, Hunt says that the good of the play is found not in Marlowe's scornfulness but in his ability in several small places to achieve "a refined sweetness."[14] This evaluation is misleading, however, because neither "monotonous" nor "sweet" are terms that seem descriptive of Marlowe's blank verse in *Tamburlaine*.

Similarly, when discussing *The Jew of Malta*, Hunt speaks of Marlowe's understanding of the "beauty of words" and his ability to reflect beauty "through the feeling of the ideas." He avoids, however, the play's theme of human greed and the fact that, while it condemns all factions, Christian and Turk, it is specifically anti-Semitic. Hunt continues by excerpting a passage from the play and instructing the reader to direct attention to its words and images instead of to Barabas's greed.[15]

Hunt's lack of comprehensiveness, therefore, may be explained by the fact that his work is an effort to depoliticize Marlowe in criticism (much like Horne had done in fiction) in order to use the playwright as fodder for a growing resistance to what he sees as the insensitive utilitarianism of the machine age. Yet, of the four major plays, only two seem to conflict with this interpretation of Marlowe. He excerpts certain "meanings" from Marlowe, therefore, in much the same way as his counterparts in the academy. His end, however, was not to make Marlowe suitable for students but to achieve almost the exact opposite effect by demonstrating that the playwright was essentially a socially conscious romantic rebel.[16]

While the understanding of Marlowe as a radical never gained wide acceptance among either educators or the literati, the romantic features of his fictionalized death accommodated the view of Marlowe that came to prominence during the second half of the nineteenth century. Bullen's reprint of Horne's play in his 1885 edition of Marlowe's *Works* (without the dedication to Hunt) removed it from its radical context and made it accessible to the late-century critics. Because it portrayed Marlowe as classically educated but ingenuous, the play drew attention from other well-educated creative thinkers who, because they became so devoted to the principles of romantic idealism, tried to turn Marlowe into an object of worship.

The Apollonian Marlowe

In order to gain a clear understanding of how Marlowe was treated by the literati after the 1870s, it is necessary to return for a moment to Dowden's critical position. Essentially, in Dowden's view, Marlowe's life and works were yet another example of high romanticism in literary history, although his assumptions were based on spurious evidence. Nonetheless, Dowden found the interpretative latitude to moralize Marlowe and to make the playwright an essential component of literary study. However, he does note that Marlowe's idealism was of a "decidedly Satanic school." This and his reference to a cult of Marlowe in his own time hint that there were views of the playwright's life and works that were neither morally doctrinaire nor suitable for the academy.[17]

Although inventive, Dowden's interpretations of Marlowe were far more cautious than those of several of his contemporaries who were not inhibited by the austere restraints of academe. Dowden, for instance, was compelled to condemn what he saw as the dark features of the pre-Shakespeareans, including Marlowe, by calling them "Satanic." What other critics did, however, was to pit what Dowden and others saw as Marlowe's dark side against Victorian moral judgment and in fact idealize these supposedly sinful attitudes. Moreover, Marlowe was interpreted in the light of an ardent but ephemeral neo-Hellenism that became a vogue among the latter-century literati. Several of these critics even used what they saw to be Marlowe's artistic temperament as an affirmation of their own unconventional life-styles.

Swinburne's criticism is a perfect point of departure in a consideration of the "other side" of Dowden's moral Marlowe. Although Swinburne seems to associate Marlowe with a variety of classical and Continental traditions, his description of the playwright's verse, like Dowden's, extolls the virtues of its high romanticism.

> In Marlowe the passion of ideal love for the ultimate idea of beauty in art or nature found its perfect and supreme expression, faultless and unforced. The radiance of his desire, the light and the flame of his aspiration, diffused and shed through all the forms of his thought and all the colours of his verse, gave them such shapeliness and strength of life as is given to the spirits of the greatest poets alone.[18]

Dowden and Swinburne both sought to promote a renewed and liberated poetic spirit during their time, and they both were ardent admirers of what they saw to be the exuberant artistic spirit of the Renaissance. Moreover, they both risked an appreciation of fresh and innovative artistic forms such as the imagistic and undisciplined verse of Walt Whitman (although Swinburne later retracted with hostility). However, unlike Dowden, Swinburne was a professional poet and his literary perspectives were shaped by a poetic theory that celebrated Hellenic literary forms and models with an uncommon zeal. Moreover, Swinburne saw the creative impulse as being the most sublime of all human endeavors. For him, literary history was a narrative of individual epic struggles undergone by a handful of heroic poets. Indeed, Swinburne saw these great poets as being no less in stature than classical deities.[19]

In a review of William Poel's 1896 production of *Dr. Faustus*, the often cantankerous G. B. Shaw said of Swinburne that he "expresses in verse what he finds in books as passionately as a poet expressed what he finds in life."[20] This was an unfair jab at Swinburne's erudition (and also at Marlowe whom Shaw calls "a blank verse beast"), but it does call up a distinct feature of the poet's understanding of Marlowe. Similar to Horne, Swinburne loses all sense of a real-life Marlowe and instead incorporates the playwright into the same stratum of fiction held by the playwright's own characters. For instance, Swinburne, in his series of sonnets on English dramatists, writes that Marlowe was

> Crowned, girdled, garbed and shod with light and fire,
> Son first-born of the morning, sovereign star![21]

This portrayal of the playwright can only be said to be the product of an overcharged imagination.

Swinburne, however, remained adamant about this extraordinary interpretation of Marlowe throughout his life. He expands on the sentiments of his sonnet in his critical introduction to his edition of the works of George Chapman (1875). After a lofty appraisal of Chapman's continuation of "Hero and Leander," Swinburne finally says that "the poet was not alive, among all the mighty men then living, who could worthily have completed the divine fragment of Marlowe."[22] He even deifies Marlowe by alluding to the final lines of "Hero and Leander," in which the poet evokes the image of Apollo's harp summoning the dawn after Hero appears naked before Leander. Indeed, these lines seem to be the source of Swinburne's infatuation with Marlowe.

> So *Heroes;* ruddie cheeke *Hero* betrayd,
> And her all naked to his sight displayd,
> Whence his admiring eyes more pleasure tooke
> Than *Dis*, on heaps of gold fixing his looke.
> By this *Apollos* golden harpe began
> To sound foorth musicke to the Ocean,
> Which watchfull *Hesperus* no sooner heard,
> But he the day bright-bearing Car prepar'd,
> And ran before, as Harbenger of light,
> And with his flaring beames mockt ougly night,
> Till she o'recome with anguish shame, and rage,
> Dang'd downe to hell her loathsome carriage.[23]

Evidently, Swinburne interpreted the entrance of Apollo as a personification of Marlowe's own imagination evoking the dawn not just of the mythical world of his poem but of the eternal romantic spirit in all English verse.

With a hyperbolic assertiveness that was typically Swinburnian, he pronounces Marlowe the avatar of English poetry by saying that the poet/playwright was "the Apollo of our dawn, the bright and morning star of the full midsummer day of English poetry at its highest."[24] Thus Marlowe is expanded into a type of cosmic abstraction whose features, both poetical and biographical, are no longer really discernible from those of a mythical God.

Shaw's criticism of Swinburne mentioned above was directed

chiefly toward the prologue Swinburne wrote for Poel's *Faustus*. The verse is characteristic of Swinburne in that he evokes wildly imaginative images within a formal poetic structure. It is also Swinburne's poetic effort to overcome the influence of his subject by attempting to be more Marlovian than Marlowe himself.

> Light, as when dawn takes wind and smites the sea,
> Smote England when his day bade Marlowe be.
> No fire so keen had thrilled the clouds of time
> Since Dante's breath made Italy sublime.
> Earth, bright with flowers whose dew shone soft as tears,
> Through Chaucer cast her charm on eyes and ears:
> The lustrous laughter of the love-lit earth
> Rang, leapt, and lightened in his might of mirth.
> Deep moonlight, hallowing all the breathless air,
> Made earth and heaven for Spenser faint and fair.
> But song might bid not heaven and earth be one
> Till Marlowe's voice gave warning of the sun.[25]

Swinburne bestows upon real poets—Dante, Chaucer, Spenser, and Marlowe—certain larger-than-life powers in much the same way that an epic poet might characterize fictional deities. To the playwright he again ascribes the classical features of Apollo: Marlowe is the poet of light and truth. This is an odd characterization because, before Swinburne, Marlowe's example had been considered more Dionysian or Epicurean than anything else.

As a result of Swinburne's effort to make an epic of English literary history, Marlowe's historical placement is conspicuously high; no one before Swinburne had ever ventured to suggest that the playwright held a position above Chaucer and Spenser. Marlowe's luminous placement in the lineage of Dante also seems overly generous during a time when even the playwright's greatest admirers usually provided him only a limited amount of space in secondary discussions of pre-Shakespearean drama.

Moreover, Swinburne's great appreciation for his predecessor stems from only several relatively small verse sections in Marlowe's plays and of course from the "divine fragment" of "Hero and Leander." While this may seem like unfirm grounds on which to hold Marlowe so highly, Swinburne obviously placed the uplifting but intemperate drive of Marlowe's imagination over the narrative refinement of a

Chaucer or a Spenser. Moreover, considering the nature of Swinburne's own infamous life-style, he was no doubt drawn to Marlowe by the rumors and speculations about the playwright's own excesses. Perhaps most important, he saw in Marlowe a general annunciation of a new era of English poetry—a historical mirror of what was perhaps Swinburne's greatest hope for his own verse.

Regardless of Swinburne's motives, which were complex and often inconsistent, the poet provided a portrait of Marlowe that seems ridiculously exaggerated and incongruous with anything we have since come to understand about the playwright's life and works. Nonetheless, his great appreciation for Marlowe does explain how the playwright may have initially become a cult. Perhaps purposefully, Swinburne's Marlowe was everything the academic's Marlowe was not. The late nineteenth-century educator, through a complex manipulation of factual and speculative evidence, moralized Marlowe and gave priority to his one drama that seemed to reaffirm Victorian religious beliefs. Swinburne, on the other hand, used his imagined Marlowe to scandalize the literary community. He was entirely unconcerned with Marlowe's biography, however, saying only that he was "a poor scholar of humblest parentage." On no authority other than his imagination, he presented Marlowe as a pagan deity and stated that when he died he went to a classical not Christian underworld.[26] Thus Marlowe was made to seem an abstract poetic presence whose life and work subverted Christian morality, and for that matter Victorian literary and social conventions.

L'Amour de l'Impossible

John Addington Symonds played a crucial role in cultivating the Hellenic vision of Marlowe that had come to fruition through the criticism of Swinburne. Also, he further contributed to the aura of controversy that constantly surrounded Marlowe's life and works. It is difficult now to see how Symonds's refined criticism could merit controversy, however, without a closer look into his lifelong passion to express freely and openly his sexual desires. As Havelock Ellis later discovered, Symonds was the quintessential Victorian case study in closet behavior. He persistently bordered on open admission of his homosexuality and even entertained the notion of publicly contending the stern laws against this practice in England during his time. As his literary criticism demonstrates, however, Symonds was more of an aesthetician than he was an activist.

His sexual frustrations, however, are well documented by scores of letters that he wrote to friends and associates during his life. There was, for instance, his now famous correspondence with Walt Whitman in which he gradually tried to pin down the American poet on the exact implications of his *Calumus* poems, becoming bolder and more succinct in each letter. The fact that Whitman ultimately demurred greatly embarrassed Symonds, who had hoped that he was witnessing in America the dawn of a new age of sexual expression.[27]

Symonds's solicitation of Whitman was just one of many frustrated attempts to come to terms with his "sexual inversion," as it was then called. Symonds himself wavered between seeing his own sexuality either as a mental illness or as a perfectly natural expression of desire. Eventually, though, he began to believe that his "un-Victorian" desires were in fact fueled by the austere social conventions of his era. This sociosexual theory guided him toward the consideration of literatures in which sexual passions were freely expressed. Thus he was intensely drawn to Greek philosophy and poetry, and at times he would voice his anger over how educators suppressed or bowdlerized the individual meanings of Greek words in their translations.

Symonds was also attracted by Swinburne's rebelliousness but, like almost everyone else who knew the poet, was eventually put off by his contemporary's arrogance and erratic literary tastes. Grosskurth, however, calls Symonds "an amorphous, unsettled creature" as a young man, who actually admired "colorful people like Swinburne who were not afraid to assert their personalities." Later they shared some common literary interests and corresponded for years in what has been termed "an amiable artificiality." Their relationship ended in 1887, however, when Swinburne hostilely denounced Whitman.[28]

For a while, though, common ground for both Swinburne and Symonds was found in their appreciation of the passionate spirit of Renaissance poetry—a spirit that they both likened to that of the classical age. Of course Marlowe's work was among the finest examples of the sensibility that Symonds admired in Renaissance literature, and his views on the playwright in fact echoed Swinburne's sentiments in his *Shakspeare's Predecessors in the English Drama* (1884). The format and often even the tone of this work is not unlike that of other historical surveys that were used by teachers and students of the Renaissance. Indeed, in places Symonds's Marlowe seems fashioned much like the moral, romantic Marlowe of the academy.

> When, therefore, we style Marlowe the father and founder of English dramatic poetry, we mean that he perceived the capacities for noble art inherent in the Romantic Drama, and proved its adaptation to high purpose by his practice.[29]

This reads like any other status quo opinion of Marlowe during this time. There were some problems, however, in Symonds's attempt to trace the origins of English drama to Marlowe, whom he regarded as providing the apex of dramatic poetry before Shakespeare.

Symonds's debt to Swinburne was in fact too profound for him to provide what would be received as a completely "sound" survey of Marlowe's life and work. He repeats Swinburne's citation of Goethe's laudatory reflection on *Faustus* ("How greatly it is all planned!"), and restates Swinburne's contention that Marlowe's characters were "the embodiments or exponents of single qualities and simple forces."[30] Symonds later cites Swinburne's most notorious comments on Marlowe almost verbatim, and he even attempts to indicate that Swinburne's assessment of Marlowe's work was also the opinion of Marlowe's contemporaries:

> Marlowe's contemporaries hailed in him a morning star of song, and marked him out as the young Apollo of his age.[31]

After quoting verses from Chapman, Peele, and Drayton, which only vaguely support this notion, he finally provides the source of his reflections on Marlowe by saying that the "most impassioned singer of our own day, Charles Algernon Swinburne, has scattered the roses and lilies of high-sounding verse and luminous prose upon that poet's [Marlowe's] tomb."[32]

Considering that Symonds here has overindulged Marlowe with the sentiments of his sometime mentor, it is no wonder that his works met with harsh reviews. The vociferous educator, Churton Collins, was particularly adamant, contending that Symonds was too given to extravagance and hyperbolic generalizations.[33] Symonds's indebtedness to Swinburne, however, was not all that offended his literary peers because it seems that Symonds also projected his own sexual desires onto the life of Marlowe. Similar to Swinburne, Symonds was moved by what he saw as the amorphous idealization of passion in the "Hero and Leander" fragment. Symonds, however, with less than his usual subtlety, interrupts an academic discussion of Marlowe by proposing what he calls a "catch-word" for Marlowe's poetry, which he says is "L'Amour de l'Impossible—the love or lust of unattainable things." According to Symonds, this catchword of the Impossible Amour is thrust by Marlowe himself, in

> the pride of his youthful insolence and lawlessness of spiritual lust, upon the most diffident and sober of his critics. Desire for the impossible— impossible not because it transcends human appetite or capacity, but because it exhausts human faculties in the infinite pursuit—this is the region of Marlowe's sway as poet.[34]

Symonds here surpasses even Swinburne in the ability to effect a type of therapy through his reading of literature. While one can accept notions of Marlowe's lawlessness and even the idea that Marlowe's characters may in fact furnish clues about the playwright's private beliefs, it is obvious that Symonds here is saying more about the "thrust" of his own lawless passions in a "diffident and sober" society. In fact, the focus of his concern is not how Marlowe rebelled against the authorities of his age but how Marlowe might be used to demonstrate the necessity for the open expression of sexual passions in Symonds's own time.

Symonds proceeds by stating that this impossible lust is "suggested by his [Marlowe's] soul's revolt against the given order of the world." This is perhaps true, but as Symonds continues, his reader finds that he has displaced his own urge to revolt in the personality he ascribes to Marlowe. Because the nature of this revolt is specifically sexual and therefore taboo, Symonds resorts to using abstract but highly sensual imagery to describe Marlowe's aesthetic consciousness. He draws a curious analogy, for instance, between Marlowe's "Titanic" characters "into whom [Marlowe] has infused his spirit" and a glass blower who blows "through the glass-pipe . . . life-breath into a bubble, permanent so long as the fine vitreous form endures."[35]

While on the surface Symonds is describing the relationship between craftmanship and artistic accomplishment, one understands that this spiritual exhaustion indicates a physical progress as well.

Symonds's imagery—the tubular infusion, the relation between the Titan and the vitreous bubble—when taken for its physical implications, is clearly marking a type of sexual exchange that occurs between the artist and his art.

He extends this analogy by saying that the glassblower, like Marlowe's characters, "thirsts for things beyond man's grasp, not merely because these things exhaust man's faculties in the pursuit, but also because the full fruition of them has been interdicted." Thus, while describing the ultimate aesthetic frustration of the artist, Symonds indicates that the exhaustion and interdiction to which he refers also signal the depletion of physical desires as well.

Symonds finishes this metaphorical digression by saying that

> Marlowe's lust for the impossible, the lust he has injected like a molten fluid into all his eminent dramatic personalities, is a desire for joys conceived by the imagination, floating within the boundaries of will and sense at some fixed moment, but transcending these firm limitations, luring the spirit onward, exhausting the corporeal faculties, engaging the soul itself in a strife with God.[36]

While his notions concerning the transcendence of art would have been acceptable, Symonds's diction calls up some licentious images. The allegory of intercourse that he maintains here is obvious: Marlowe as artist conceived his characters through the injection of a lust that, like a molten fluid, exceeds "firm limitations." This act, too, is transcendent and ultimately divine.

Symonds conspicuously avoids all discussion of *Edward II* within his concept of Marlowe's lust for the impossible. Indeed, Edward's passion for Gaveston is a curious omission when Symonds in fact points out the desires of Leander, Tamburlaine, Barabas, Faustus, and even Guise to exemplify his point. This, however, is typical of Symonds as he wanders dangerously close to a transgression in places and then recants with thinly disguised rhetorical tactics.

In Symonds's defense, however, the lifelong theme of his criticism was that great literature was written by free spirits who were not afraid to challenge either poetic or social conventions. He agreed with Swinburne that Marlowe was the premier example from a group of Renaissance poets who fit this description. Symonds's affected style, therefore, is the result of his great desire to illuminate what he found as the exemplary human passions expressed by historical authors to a socially reserved and sexually conservative intellectual community.

He ends his survey of Shakespeare's predecessors by quoting the Chorus from the final scene of *Faustus,* thus providing a trace of the thread of literary thought that held his "school" together.

> Cut is the branch that might have grown full straight,
> And burned is Apollo's laurel bough,
> That sometime grew within this learned man.[37]

These lines are of course directed toward the fallen hero in *Faustus,* but, as Symonds reminds the reader, they were also borrowed by Horne who made them Middleton's final comment on the death of Christopher Marlowe.

This small point is crucial to the understanding of just how Horne, Swinburne, and Symonds came to see Marlowe as a fictional "character" whose early death mirrored the demise of his own tragic heroes. Instead of viewing Marlowe as unrighteous and corrupt, however, they saw the playwright's passionate works and untimely death as the ephemeral destiny of a "poet of light" who gave up his life for his art. As Swinburne argued, his soul was not the victim of Christian demons but was instead consigned to the underworld with Homer and Orpheus. While these are seemingly wild and exotic ideas that do not seem to have solid footing in reality, they are essentially sensational challenges to Victorian social and literary conventions and not serious attempts to present an accurate view of history.

Marlowe and Sexual Inversion

One of the ways in which the methods of literary interpretation gained a foothold in the social sciences during the late nineteenth and early twentieth centuries was through the work of the famous sexologist Havelock Ellis. Although much of his research has since been eclipsed by the work of Freud, he enjoyed a wide reputation during his time as being the depraved and degenerate author of several semiempirical works that openly analyzed the psychology of sexual repression.[38] His biographers, however, tend to portray him as an eccentric but kind man who was thoroughly open-minded but generally shy and ascetic.[39] He shared with Freud, though, a relentless desire to expose the underlying sexual neuroses that he felt were provoked by the strict moral and social conventions of his era. Considering the cultural environment in which Ellis published case studies on such subjects as pederasty and lesbianism, it is little wonder that he was generally received as a hybrid of Lucifer and Don Juan.

Among a select circle of enlightened insiders, however, Ellis enjoyed as a young man a reputation as a humanist and as a refined and knowledgeable literary critic. His importance to this discussion is rooted more in his early "literary" concerns, although these were inextricably tied to what he later attempted to establish as a sexologist. Specifically, he was the first to argue that Marlowe had all of the characteristics of a "sexual invert." He attempted to put forth this theory, though, not for moral reproof or sensation, but as part of an argument that homosexuality was a historical and therefore "natural" human phenomenon that was especially common among artists. Marlowe, therefore, became part of Ellis's effort to attack the Victorian sexual conventions that repressed what he found to be the essential passions of the artistic temperament.

Although sympathetic to the romantic methodology used by Dowden, Ellis, like Taine, was more an offspring of late nineteenth-century empiricism than he was a literary aesthete. Using case studies rather than literary analysis, for instance, he pointed out that most sexual inverts have an "artistic aptitude," which includes a "taste for music" and certain dramatic talents.[40] He was compelled, therefore, to place Marlowe in this category of free artistic spirits whose visions and meanings had been suppressed by the Victorian critical mind.

In his autobiography Ellis makes it clear that his early appreciation of Marlowe and the playwright's contemporaries was fueled by Swinburne and even to a greater extent by Symonds. In fact, on both the subjects of sexuality and Marlowe, Ellis collaborated with Symonds, who eventually became one of Ellis's soul mates in his effort to publish a form of scientific discourse on the psychology of sexual repression. Their association began after Ellis's favorable review of Symonds's *The Renaissance in Italy* (1885), when the younger Ellis received a letter from Symonds complimenting him on his frankness and insight. For several years, the two corresponded, and they eventually agreed to produce a treatise on sexuality that would provide both an empirical and historical overview of alternative sexual behavior.

During the same period, Ellis had contacted the publisher Henry Vizetelly, who attracted Ellis's attention and admiration because he had the nerve to publish "fairly" literal translations of some of the more controversial French novelists.[41] At the time, Ellis was determined to make what he saw to be the best achievements of the Renaissance dramatists accessible, "in such a way that the finest of all were not omitted for the sake of some absurd prudery."[42] Ellis cited the conspicuous omission of Ford's 'Tis Pity She's a Whore from editions of the playwright's work as an example of the stringent regard for propriety that editors had during this period.

Invoking what he saw as the open and spirited literary ambiance of the old Mermaid tavern, Ellis proposed to Vizetelly that an unexpurgated series of Renaissance dramatists should be completed under that name.[43] Vizetelly responded by offering the general editorship of the Mermaid series to the then twenty-seven-year old Ellis. It was also understood that the series would be provided at a reasonable cost (the 1850 Dyce and 1885 Bullen editions were relatively high priced) and that it would seek to inform a more popular market of the true spirit of the drama by providing works and information that had been subdued by prior editors.

But Ellis was not really a Renaissance scholar; he was a widely read social reformer. Therefore, he was not as interested in establishing a clear bibliographical record for Renaissance authors as he was in using these figures to induce a type of social shock treatment for a culture that he felt was overcome by notions of social propriety and sexual modesty. Essentially, he saw the Mermaid series as the inauguration of what would be a lifelong incumbency to expose and distinguish a "New Spirit" of late-century literary and thus social attitudes.[44] The Renaissance provided, in Ellis's view, an artistic freedom that had been reawakened by the romantics and that was coming of age in philosophically progressive and creative works of writers such as Tolstoy, Flaubert, and Whitman.

At first the Mermaid series sounds as if it were a poorly conceived attempt to scandalize English history by providing uncensored versions of Renaissance drama for a popular audience. Ellis, however, was an adept critic who, although contentious, had what was then considered good taste. He was also clever enough to bring prestige to his series by asking the controversial but noteworthy Renaissance critics Swinburne and Symonds to provide introductions for Middleton and Marlowe, respectively. (He also asked a then "young unknown writer" by the name of Arthur Symons to undertake Massinger.)

The Mermaid series began in 1887 with an edition of Marlowe edited and introduced by Ellis, with Symonds providing a prefatory general introduction. The *Mermaid Marlowe* is the ultimate popular readers' edition to the playwright's work, circumscribed as it is by ornate Arcadian engravings and cultivated introductory discussions. Because of its attractiveness, the edition was reprinted frequently and is regarded today as a collector's item. To echo the sentiments of a fashion designer, "it makes a statement" about a literary environment still concerned with the pursuit of beauty and truth and yet unspoiled by the rigors of literary research. For the modern reader, there is nothing about the *Mermaid Marlowe* that could be considered scandalous or even shocking. However, when one takes a closer look at the mood in which it was published, it becomes clear that Ellis did indeed present a Marlowe who could not be tolerated even by the most flamboyant members of the literary community.

Considering Symonds's earlier rapture over the subject of Marlowe, his introduction is comparatively tame and brief. However, the fact that Symonds's name had by then become associated with the new Hellenistic affront to conventional letters provides a sufficient signal that Marlowe had fallen into the hands of the literary avant-garde. Symonds's tempered and informative introduction, moreover, seems to be part of a general Fabian strategy that Ellis uses to submit a radicalized version of Marlowe to a popular audience.

A close reading of Ellis's observations on Marlowe reveals that he manipulates the playwright's biography in much the same way as educators did before him. Like Symonds, for instance, his discussion of Marlowe in places re-sounds the tones of academe. He begins his discussion of the life of Marlowe by emphasizing the spirit of reform that had overtaken the Canterbury of Marlowe's youth.

Early in the sixteenth century Erasmus, accompanied by Colet, visited Canterbury. Long afterwards he remembered the cathedral and its vast towers that rise into the sky "so as to strike awe even at a distant approach," the sweet music of the bells heard from afar, the "spacious majesty" of the newly completed nave. Here, fifty years later, was born Christopher, sometime called Kit, Marlowe.

Ellis here is well within the boundaries of creative license afforded even the most austere educators during his time. However, as he continues his discussion, Ellis draws analogies that his peers in education might consider improper. He goes on to say that

> the spirit of Erasmus, and still more the ruder spirit of Colet, had heralded a revolutionary influx of new life. At the head of the movement was set by Providence, in a mood of Rabelaisian gaiety, the figure of Henry VIII. Like another Tamburlaine, Henry VIII had carried off the rich treasures of Canterbury, the gold and the jewels, in six- and-twenty carts.[45]

These observations may have presented some problems for the late nineteenth-century academic. The notion of the early church reform-ers as providing a "revolutionary influx of new life," considering the then current sociopolitical implications of the word "revolution," might have been thought a misunderstanding of the ultimate social goals of Erasmus and Colet. Moreover, the suggestion that Provi-dence set up Henry "in a mood of Rabelaisian gaiety" would not compliment the personality and temperament that the Victorians generally assigned to God. Also, while no one would argue that Henry did not have a dark side, the figure of the king as a Tamburlaine-like ruler who by inference seized the treasures of Canterbury like a power-mad heathen would certainly not please any defenders of the rights of royal authority.

It is evident that Ellis is exploiting the latitudes that high roman-ticism allowed the Victorian literary critic so that he can draw parallels between the age of Elizabeth and what he sees as the dawn of a new spirit during his own age. However, he romanticizes Marlowe not to adapt the playwright to the moral mandates of the Victorian academy but to provide a historical adversary to Victorian convention.

For instance, Ellis's primary source was Bullen's 1885 edition of Marlowe's works, one that is uncommonly accurate for the period in which it was produced. In his overview of the life of Marlowe, however, Ellis departs or at least diverts attention from Bullen's research at several key points in much the same way that earlier historians had manipulated the research of Broughton, Collier, and

Dyce. Although Bullen clearly asserts that Marlowe's dramatic career was based on hearsay and forgery, Ellis remarks that this prospect had been forwarded "by the unsupported evidence of a late and often inaccurate authority." One is not sure whether or not Ellis is referring to Collier or to Edward Phillips, who, writing over eighty years after Marlowe's death, was the first to contend that Marlowe had appeared on the boards. Bullen had carefully distinguished both sources and noted their tenuousness. Ellis, however, seems to be veiling the existing research in order to maintain, on the power of suggestion, the possibility that Marlowe was an actor. Like so many before him, Ellis may have preferred a Marlowe with an actor's temperament.

Ellis also avoids the many specific accounts of Marlowe's death, maintaining only the "rival lover" report from Meres as fact. Bullen, however, had printed this report as one of many speculations from Marlowe's contemporaries. Overall, Ellis sentimentalizes Marlowe's death in much the same spirit that Horne had before him.

> In May [of 1593] we know that Marlowe was at the little village of Deptford, not many miles from London. There was turbulent blood there, and wine; there were courtesans and daggers. Here Marlowe was slain, killed by a serving-man, a rival in a quarrel over bought kisses—"a bawdy serving-man."[46]

The disparity between Bullen's biography and Ellis's, written less than two years later, indicates that Ellis was, like many of his contemporaries in academe, attempting to reproduce a sentimental and highly romantic portrait of the playwright.

However, in the appendix to his edition, Ellis prints the famous Baines note in its entirety, and thus draws attention to the most damning piece of evidence against the playwright's character. While the note was well known among Marlowe scholars, it had been securely protected from the public eye in the nineteenth century. Sections of the note had been printed on occasion, and Dyce had even published a bowdlerized version of it in his own appendix.[47]

No one in the nineteenth century, however, had printed several key statements that Baines had accused Marlowe of making. Unlike researchers before him, Ellis did not question Baines's reliability, who, as several biographers noted, had been hanged at Tyburn. In fact, in his introduction, Ellis holds that "there seems no reason—while

making judicious reservations—to doubt the substantial accuracy of
his [Baines's] statements." By trying to print a censored version of this
manuscript, Ellis was definitely not attempting to moralize Marlowe.
In fact, he provided the most scandalous view of the playwright
during the Victorian period.

It is ironic that the very critics who inspired Ellis to be more
adventurous in the interpretation of Renaissance drama were also
agents in having the Baines note suppressed. Somehow Vizetelly, the
ardent publisher of risqué novels, was motivated to censor the note
just after the first edition of the *Mermaid Marlowe* went into print.
According to Peterson, the reason that the printer substituted as-
terisks for several of Baines's accusations was because a "well-meaning
woman" protested to the note.[48] In his autobiography, however, Ellis
indicates there were other reasons. About the early copies that included the most notorious blasphemies, Ellis says that

> many people were shocked, including even Swinburne and J. A. Sy-
> monds, who were both taking part in my scheme, and they both wrote to
> tell me of their disapproval, while Vizetelly, without even consulting me,
> swiftly mutilated my appendix.[49]

Thus one assumes that among the scandalized were the scan-
dalmongers themselves. Neither Swinburne nor Symonds wished to
expose the public to Baines's note because it conflicted with their
ideal Marlowe whom they had championed as the avatar of English
verse.

No one, however, censored the conclusions that Ellis drew around
Marlowe in *Sexual Inversion* (1897). Swinburne had no influence on
the publication of this project because it was primarily nonliterary.
And although the work was conceived as a collaborative exercise
between Symonds and Ellis, Symonds had little to say about that final
product because he had recently died.[50] While this work was primarily a quasi-scientific discussion of pederasty and lesbianism, it also
had a literary flare in Symonds's review of the origins of sexual
inversion, specifically in his essay on the problem of Greek ethics.
Moreover, both Ellis and Symonds seemed especially intent on furnishing numerous historical examples of great women and men who
were sexual inverts.

In his introduction, Ellis contends that "in modern Europe we find the strongest evidence of the presence of what may fairly be called true sexual inversion when we investigate the men of the Renaissance." His list includes Michelangelo and Bazzi, of the Italian school, and Marlowe among the English (he falls just short of indicating Shakespeare). Citing from Baines, Marlowe's alledged assertion that "all they that loue not Tobacco & Boies were fooles" (see Appendix B), Ellis says that Marlowe "clearly had a reckless delight in all things unlawful, and it seems probable that he possessed the psychosexual hermaphrodite's [bisexual's] temperament."[51]

While Ellis was too scientifically blunt about Marlowe's alleged sexual preferences for the aesthetician who wished to mystify the poet, he drew his ideas from a literati who had furnished Marlowe with the laurels and sensual presence of an Arcadian deity. Swinburne (and to a degree Horne) directly influenced Symonds, and Symonds directly influenced Ellis. As a result, Marlowe was passed through the hands of a circle of thinkers who made him perhaps the most outrageous figure in English literary history by the end of the century. Thus Ellis provided the epitome of a strain of thought that fueled even new critical speculation about Marlowe's sexuality well into the twentieth century.

Unlike the Victorian educator, the literati had a smaller proclivity for affecting historical accuracy. They were more concerned with the spirit of the past—a spirit that curiously mirrored and supported their own current concerns. All said, Marlowe was taken through a cycle by the literati during which he was radicalized, mystified, and worshiped. (He was by this time even considered a strong contender for Shakespeare's rival lover).[52] By the 1890s, considering the variety of interpretive efforts that had been contributed to the playwright's life and works, it is little wonder that he was deemed to be everything from the most moral to the most wicked of the Renaissance playwrights.

The result of the clash between the academic Marlowe and the Marlowe of the literati seemed to draw even more attention to the playwright, making him somewhat of a vogue during the nineties. Marlowe was taken up by the literary societies, and there were several more works that portrayed him as a literary subject.[53] There was even a Marlowe Memorial (which Tucker Brooke describes as "tasteless") erected in Canterbury. By the end of the century, the same playwright who had been virtually ignored by the literary communmity less than a hundred years earlier had reached prominence not through a consistent or organized critical effort but as a result of the multifarious manipulations of his life and work by researchers and critics who had a wide variety of social and political concerns. After one examines the views of these critics and the effect that they had on the literary community, it becomes obvious that the "demonic" Marlowe to which the drunk and overwrought Hart Crane likened himself was not the author of a handful of sixteenth-century plays and poems but a completely reformed product of nineteenth-century letters.

Conclusion

MY primary objective during this study has been to demonstrate how the biography and artistic motives of a Renaissance playwright were essentially invented by nineteenth-century critics. There is also abundant evidence that twentieth-century studies have suffered as the result of a type of intellectual annexation from this specifically nineteenth-century discursive field. This work owes a great debt to two important bibliographical essays that make this point. Both of these deserve some specific attention as a way of further demonstrating the enormous influence that nineteenth-century letters has had on Marlowe studies during this century.

Millar Maclure, in *Marlowe: The Critical Heritage* (1979), provides key excerpts from many of the nineteenth-century critics who were covered in this study. In his introduction, Maclure insists that although "critical tools have been sharpened" in this century, the tendency to view Marlowe's plays and poems solely as "expressions of the personality of their maker" did not "disappear with Ellis and Swinburne."[1] Although few scholars are now naive enough to make a major biographical point either from spurious information or from the playwright's renderings of various dramatic and poetic themes, certain crucial biographical points are still widely accepted on little evidence. In the light of countless twentieth-century examples, it is not difficult to concur with Maclure's observation that the interpretation of Marlowe's life and works are still tainted by a theory of art that was established by the nineteenth-century man of letters.

The second bibliographical essay that marks the persistent influence of nineteenth-century interpretations of Marlowe on twentieth-century scholarship is Kenneth Friedenreich's introduction to *Christopher Marlowe: An Annotated Bibliography of Criticism since 1950* (1979). Entitled "Marlowe Criticism and *On the Origin of Species*," Friedenreich's discussion is central to this study in that he argues that twentieth-century criticism on drama is still overly influenced by a late nineteenth-century "evolutionary bias." Friedenreich goes on to

list eight specific critical commonplaces that were inherited from
Victorian scholarship and propagated throughout this century. Most of
these concern Marlowe's artistic contributions to the history of English drama. In sum, the view of Marlowe inherited by the twentieth
century was that he was a daring verse pioneer who influenced Shakespeare, and although highly inspired his plays are artistically flawed.
Behind this assessment is the ambiguous but influencial portrait of
Marlowe drawn by educators and aesthetes during the second half of
the nineteenth century.[2]

Friedenreich goes on to draw a dichotomy between two fundamental types of twentieth-century criticism, both of which were inherited
from the Victorians and both of which have persisted throughout this
century. The first is the essentially "romantic" view of Marlowe as a
subjective artist, which was reconfirmed in the work of such critics as
F. S. Boas and Una Ellis-Fermor. The second is rooted in Roy
Battenhouse's contention that Marlowe was a "more conservative,
objective artist whose plays assess Renaissance drives for power,
wealth, and knowledge." According to Friedenreich, both views have
persisted in the post–World War II period and "are only now being
systematically questioned."[3]

Friedenreich's observations on nineteenth- and twentieth-century
criticism in fact predicated the idea of conducting a more expansive
research project that would focus on the origins of certain twentieth-
century dogmas concerning the interpretation of Marlowe's life and
works. As it turns out, both the subjective Marlowe of the romantic
school and the objective Marlowe of the historical/empirical school
were indeed born during the past century. The two most apparent
examples of this critical dichotomy can be found in the influential
interpretations of Dowden, the romantic metaphysician, and Taine,
the historical determinist.

Although Friedenreich's understanding of the influence of Dyce,
Dowden, Swinburne, Ellis, and others on our views is well-informed
and feasible, one is inclined, after a closer examination, to enlarge
upon his observations. Essentially, Darwinism is not actually the
cause of certain late nineteenth-century appropriations of Marlowe's
life and work but yet another effect of certain economic and demographic changes that took place before Darwin. In Marlowe studies,
Collier, as early as 1831, was the first to suggest that Marlowe was an
essential component of a dramatic tradition that developed or

"evolved" from the Middle Ages through Shakespeare. By tracing, among other things, the history of certain repeated forgeries, this study shows how influential Collier's observations were on critics of the late nineteenth century. Therefore, Friedenreich is correct to maintain that progressivist ideas about Marlowe's historical importance were propagated by late nineteenth-century letters. However, these ideas were rooted more deeply in early nineteenth-century economic, political, and social transformations than they were in Darwinistic theory.

Using studies on Marlowe as an example, one suspects that as we approach the end of yet another century of literary research, we have not successfully established a way of talking about historical literature that is sufficiently autonomous from Victorian literary theory. Fundamentally, Marlowe has never recovered from the various and disparate turns that his biography took during the Victorian era. Moreover, his religious beliefs, his debauchery, his homosexuality are still features of his life that critics deny or defend as if they were recent issues brought up by more scientifically expansive investigations.

Our understanding of Marlowe has of course undergone some significant changes during the mid- to late twentieth century, and for the most part these newer perspectives are the result of painstaking research that uncovered fresh and valuable information. One is suspicious, however, of views that are fueled by popular trends. The understanding of Marlowe as a "secret agent," for instance, although based on intriguing evidence of his service for the queen and his associations, seems colored by a modern understanding of espionage through fictional characters such as James Bond. Similarly, there are critics who attempt to place Marlowe's life within the genre of "unsolved mysteries." Chief among these is Wraight and Stern's "In Search of" edition (1965). Although a valuable source, it treats Marlowe as if the playwright were part of an ancient mystery that had been solved by the wonders of modern scholarship. However, most of the information presented in the edition was uncovered during the nineteenth and early twentieth centuries and not during the space age.

Marlowe's image has been influenced moreover by twentieth-century literary theory. Notions of Marlowe as a modernist or postmodernist, however, are sometimes as suspicious as the Victorian understanding of Marlowe as a moral reformist or a romantic. In fact these views tend to sweep the playwright into yet another polemic established to contend with Victorian thought. For instance, the modernist Harry Levin, in his fine study of Malowe's poetics, *The Overreacher* (1957), defines Marlowe and the University Wits as members of a "lost generation."[4] This statement runs contrary to Victorians notions of the romantic Marlowe by hinting that the playwright was more of a disillusioned nihilist than an aficionado of aesthetic transcendence. However, there seems to be a vast historical difference between the sensibilities of Gertrude Stein and those of Robert Green.

More recently, Stephen Greenblatt, in *Renaissance Self-Fashioning* (1980), ends a dynamic reading of Marlowe's works with a description of Marlowe as an "estranged" subversive.

> In his turbulent life and, more important, in his writing Marlowe is deeply implicated in his heroes, though he is far more intelligent and self-aware than any of them. Cutting himself off from the comforting doctrine of repetition, he writes plays that spurn and subvert his culture's metaphysical and ethical certainties. We who have lived after Nietzsche and Flaubert may find it difficult to grasp how strong, how recklessly courageous Marlowe must have been: to write as if the admonitory purpose of literature were a lie, to invent fictions only to create and not to serve God or the state, to fashion lines that echo in the void, that echo more powerfully because there is nothing but a void. Hence Marlowe's implication in the lives of his protagonists and hence too his surmounting of this implication in the creation of enduring works of art.[5]

It could be argued that the Marlowe Greenblatt presents—the artist bravely forging human values in the face of an impersonal, abysmal universe—is not far removed from the subjective views of the playwright one routinely finds in Victorian letters. However, this type of historicism, acutely aware as it is of its own position and of the temporality of canonical texts, does serve a desperately needed function. Specifically, Greenblatt's approach to the playwright offers a corrective alternative to the hidden agendas (often couched in positivist language) that have marked studies on Marlowe.

One senses, therefore, in the historical interpretations that have been spearheaded by Greenblatt, an exciting political directness that seems more characteristic of our period than of the late nineteenth century. This directness is achieved, moreover, through a literary methodology that does not privilege certain "literary" texts and thereby push aside thousands of Renaissance documents that heretofore have been considered secondary because they were not deemed pertinent in discussions of art and theory. While one could argue that criticism concerned with such themes as the upward mobility of courtiers and sumptuary laws is only projecting a current anguish over our own preoccupation with career and fashion, many of the new historicists have at least turned to a legitimate form of literary research—one based more in bibliographical discovery than in abstract conjecture.

In closing, it would be my hope that certain more wide-reaching implications could be made from a study of this nature although one has to be careful not to infer too much. The lasting effect that Victorian interpretations have had on Marlowe calls forth questions about other Renaissance authors who ran a similar critical gauntlet. Shakespeare has already been the object of serious study in this vein. Most notably, Gary Taylor's *Reinventing Shakespeare* (1989),[6] a recent and necessary examination of Shakespeare's reception through the ages, is a strong addition to Samuel Schoenbaum's pioneering and influencial *Shakespeare's Lives* (1970). Both of these studies provide thorough examinations of the Victorian reception of Shakespeare, but neither expose to any great degree the enduring influences of Victorian literary theory on English studies today. Therefore, there is much more work that needs to be done. As many other recent studies have shown, our view of literary history is still largely guided by precepts that have seen their day. Moreover these precepts are often defended simply on the grounds that they are literary traditions. In at least the case of one Renaissance figure, however, one can see that a tradition was established by critical efforts that were often unsound and occasionally reckless. Perhaps by presenting a more accurate understanding of the critical history to which Renaissance authors have been exposed, we may be able to gain a more vital understanding of these authors and of ourselves.

Appendix A: Anthony à Wood's Account of Marlowe's Death

WOOD'S account on Marlowe is taken from his entry on Thomas Newton in his *Athenae Oxonienses* (1691). Below is Wood's account of Marlowe's death.

> But in the end, so it was, that this Marlo giving too large a swing to his own wit, and suffering his lust to have the full reins, fell to that outrage and extremity, as Jodelle a French tragical poet did, (being an epicure and an atheist,) that he denied God and his Son Christ, and not only in word blasphemed the Trinity, but also (as it was credibly* reported) wrote divers discourses against it, affirming our Saviour to be a deceiver, and Moses to be a conjurer: The holy Bible also to contain only vain and idle stories, and all religion but a device of policy. But see the end of this person, which was noted by all, especially the precisians. *For so it fell out, that he being deeply in love with a certain woman, had for his rival a bawdy serving-man, one rather fit to be a pimp, than an ingenious amoretto as Marlo conceived himself to be. Whereupon Marlo taking it to be an high affront, rush'd in upon, to stab, him, with his dagger:* But the serving-man being very quick, so avoided the stroke, that withal catching hold of Marlo's wrist, he stab'd his own dagger into his own head, in such sort, that notwithstanding all the means of surgery that could be wrought, he shortly after died of his wound, before the year 1593. (Column 9, my italics)

Appendix B: The Baines Note

IN a note from Richard Baines to the Privy Council transcribed around the time of Marlowe's death, the playwright is accused of persuading men to atheism. The two extant copies of the Baines note do not agree textually. However, the charges are similar in both. Below is the note that Kocher reprints for his analysis of Marlowe's religious thought. The accusations are presented in the supposed order in which they were made; however, the numerals indicate a proposed rearrangement to subject matter. The note was reproduced in several ways in the late eighteenth and nineteenth centuries, none of which is entirely in agreement with the one below. The accusation was used by a variety of writers to make a number of points concerning Marlowe. It was verified by those who wished to condemn Marlowe and contested by those who wished to defend him. The note was also bowdlerized, expurgated, and quoted out of context. (Angle brackets indicate discrepancies between the surviving copies.)

A note Containing the opinion of on Christopher Marly Concerning his damnable <opini> Judgment of Religion, and scorn of Gods word.

Ia   That the Indians and many Authors of antiquity haue assuredly writen of aboue 16 thousand yeares agone whereas <Moyses> Adam is <said> proued to haue lived within 6 thowsand yeares.

Ib   He affirmeth that Moyses was but a Jugler & that one Heriots being Sir W Raleighs man Can do more than he.

Id   That Moyses made the Jewes to travell xl yeares in the wildernes, (which Jorney might haue bin done in lesse than one yeare) ere they Came to the promised land to thintent that those who were privy to most of his subtilties might perish and so an everlasting superstition Remain in the hartes of the people.

Ie   That the beginning of Religioun was only to keep men in awe.

Ic   That it was an easy matter for Moyses being brought up in all the artes of the Egiptians to abuse the Jewes being a rude & grosse people.

2b   That Christ was a bastard and his mother dishonest.

2c   That he was the sonne of a Carpenter, and that if the Jewes among whome he was borne did Crucify him theie best knew him and whence he Came.

2d   That crist deserved better to dy then Barrabas and that the Jewes made a good Choise, though Barrabas were both a thief and a murtherer.

3a   That if there be any god or any good Religion, then it is in the papistes because the service of god is performed with more Cerimonies, as Elevation of the mass, organs, singing men, Shaven Crownes & cta. That all protestantes are Hypocritical asses.

3c   That if he were put to write a new Religion, he would vndertake both a more Exellent and Admirable methode and that all the new testament is filthily written.

2c   That the woman of Samaria & her sister were whores & that Crist knew them dishonestly.

2f   That St John the Evangelist was bedfellow to Christ and leaned alwaies in his bosome, that he vsed him as the sinners of Sodoma.

2g   That all they that loue not Tobacco & Boies were fooles.

3d   That all the apostles were fishermen and base fellowes neyther of wit nor worth, that Paull only had with but he was a timerous fellowe in bidding men to be subiect to magistrates against his Conscience.

3e   That he had as good Right to Coine as the Queen of England, and that he was aquainted with one Poole a prisoner in Newgate who hath greate skill in mixture of mettals and hauing learned some thinges of him he ment through help of a Cunninge stamp maker to Coin ffrench Crownes pistoletes and English shillinges.

3b   That if Christ would haue instituted the sacrament with more Ceremoniall Reverence it would haue bin in more admiration, that it would haue bin much better being administered in a Tobacco pipe.

2a   That the Angell Gabriell was baud to the holy ghost, because he brought the salutation to to Mary.

4a   That on Ric Cholmley <hath Cholmley> hath Confessed that he was perswaded by Marloe's Reasons to become an Atheist.

    These thinges, with many other shall by good & honest witnes be aproved to be his opinions and Comon Speeches and that this Marlow doth not only hould them himself, but almost into every Company he Cometh he perswades men to Atheism willing them not to be afeard

of bugbeares and hobgoblins, and vtterly scorning both god and his
ministers as I Richard Baines wil Justify & spproue both by mine oth
and the testimony of many honest men, and almost al men with
whome he hath Conversed any time will testify the same, and as I
think all men in Christianity ought to indevor that the mouth of / so
dangerous a member may be stopped, he saith likewise that he hath
quoted a number of Contrarieties oute of the Scripture which he hath
giuen to some great men who in Convenient time shalbe named.
When these thinges shalbe Called in question the witnes shalbe
produced.

Richard Baines
(Quoted from Kocher, 35–36)

Appendix C: Lamb's Excerpt from *Tamburlaine*

LAMB says that he "subjoined" the speech below for his reader's "amusement."

Enter Tamburlaine, drawn in his chariot by Trbizon and Soria, with bits in their mouths, reins in his left hand, in his right hand a whip, with which he scourgeth them.

> TAMB. Holla ye pamper'd jades of Asia:
> What can ye draw but twenty miles a day,
> And have so proud a chariot at your heels,
> And such a coachman as great Tamburlaine?
> But from Asphaltis, where I conquered you,
> To Byron here, where thus I honour you?
> The horses that guide the golden eye of heaven,
> And blow the morning from their nostrils,
> Making their fiery gate above the clouds,
> Are not so honour'd in their governor
> As you ye slaves in mighty Tamburlaine.
> The headstrong jades of Thrace Alcides tamed,
> That King Egeus fed with human flesh,
> And made so wanton that they knew their strengths,
> Were not subdued with valour more divine,
> Than you by this unconquer'd arm of mine,
> To make you fierce and fit my appetite,
> You shall be fed with flesh as raw as blood,
> And drink in pails the strongest muscadel:
> If you can live with it, then live and draw
> My chariot swifter than the racking clouds:
> If not, then die like beasts, and fit for nought
> But perches for the black and fatal ravens,
> Thus am I right the scourge of highest Jove. &c.

Notes

Introduction

1. See Tucker Brooke, "The Reputation of Christopher Marlowe," *Transactions of the Connecticut Academy of Arts and Sciences* 25 (June 1922): 347–408.
2. Michel Foucault, "What is an Author?" trans. Josue V. Harari, in *Textual Strategies: Perspectives in Post-Structuralist Criticism*, ed. Josue V. Harari (Ithaca: Cornell University Press, 1979), 147.
3. Edward Said, *Orientalism* (New York: Pantheon Books, 1978), 22.
4. Marilyn Butler, *Romantics, Rebels, and Reactionaries: English Literature and Its Background 1760–1830*, (Oxford: Oxford University Press, 1982), 1.

Chapter 1. The Discovery of Marlowe in the Early Nineteenth Century

1. William Hazlitt, *Lectures on the Age of Elizabeth*, vol. 6 in *The Complete Works of William Hazlitt*, ed. P. P. Howe (London: J. M. Dent and Sons, 1931), 6:202.
2. Brooke, "The Reputation of Christopher Marlowe," 383.
3. Ralph Straus, *Robert Dodsley: Poet, Publisher and Playwright* (London: John Lane at the Bodley Head, 1910), 65.
4. Ibid., 63–64
5. Robert Dodsley ed., *A Select Collection of Old Plays*, 1st ed., 12 vols. (London: 1744), ix. Dodsley begins his section on English theater by saying:

> I come now more particularly to consider the rise and progress of the English stage, which was the principal design of this *Preface*. It is generally, I believe, imagined, that the English stage rose later than the rest of its neighbours. Those in this opinion will, perhaps, wonder to be told of theatrical entertainments almost as early as the Conquest; and yet nothing is more certain, if you will believe an honest monk, one William Stephanides, or Fitz-Stephen, in his *Descriptio Nobilissimae Civitatis Londoniae*, who writes thus: "London, instead of common interludes belonging to the theatre, hath plays of a more holy subject; representations of those miracles which the holy confessors wrought, or of the sufferings wherein the glorious constancy of the martyrs did appear." This author was a monk of Canterbury, who wrote in the reign of Henry II and died in that of Richard I, 1191: and as he does not mention these representations as novelties to the people (for he is describing all the common diversions in use at that time), we can hardly fix them lower than the Conquest. And this, I believe, is an earlier date than any other nation of Europe can produce for their theatrical representations.

6. Ibid., xvii–xxx.
7. Robert Dodsley, ed., *Old Plays*, 2d ed. (London: J. Nichols for J. Dodsley, 1780), ix.
8. Thomas Beard, *The Theatre of God's Judgement* (London: Islip and Spark, 1631), lib. 1, chap. xxv.

9. Anthony à Wood, *Athenae Oxonienses,* ed. Philip Bliss (1691; reprint, London: Rivington et al., 1815), vol. 2, cols. 7–9.

10. It should be mentioned that after Dodsley repeated Wood's account (1691), someone, probably a man named Robert Shiels (see Brooke, "Reputation," 387), does add some positive remarks about Marlowe in Cibber's *Lives of the Poets* (1753) by reporting his Cambridge education and certain positive evaluations of his poetry by Jonson and Heywood. He also hints that Marlowe was affiliated with Shakespeare (Cibber, 85–87). Wood's negative reports of Marlowe's life, though, remained influencial throughout the eighteenth and nineteenth centuries. See also Bishop Thomas Tanner, whose *Bibliotheca Britannico-Hibernia* (1748; fac. reprint, Tucson: Aucax Press, 1963) notes Marlowe's Cambridge education (512) but basically repeats Wood.

11. Thomas Wharton, *The History of English Poetry from the Close of the Eleventh to the Commencement of the Eighteenth Century,* vol. 4 (London: Ward, Lock, and co., 1781), 260.

12. Ibid., 265.

13. Joseph Ritson, "Observations on the Three First Volumes of the *History of English Poetry,* a Familiar Letter to the Author" (London: J. Stockdale, 1782), entry addressing vol. 4, p. 437 of Warton's work.

14. This would be the only printing of an unexpurgated version of the Baines note until Ellis's 1887 edition, in which the note was presented in an appendix but changed even before the first printing was finished. The Baines libel was mentioned on many occasions throughout the nineteenth century, however, most notably by Dyce, Taine, and Ellis (see Appendix B).

15. An odd irony concerning Ritson's moral zeal is that, according to the *Dictionary of National Biography,* in 1791, after a visit to Paris he adopted whole-heartedly the republican doctrine of the French revolutionaries and publically declared himself an atheist.

16. Brooke, "Reputation," 390.

17. Charles Lamb, *Specimens of English Dramatic Poets Who Lived About the Time of Shakespeare* (London: Longman, Hurst, Rees, Orme, 1808).

18. Ibid., v.

19. Ibid., 15–40.

20. Ibid., vi.

21. Ibid., 40.

22. Ibid., 17.

23. Ibid., 19.

24. This "madness," when understood in terms of the insanity that was so prevalent in Lamb's own family, may be precisely what inspired him to interpret the text in this manner.

25. Lamb was apparently consulting a British Museum copy of *Tamburlaine.* The play survived in several early editions that were released from 1590 through 1606. It was not edited, printed, and released again until the 1818–20 Oxberry serial edition of Marlowe's works. One assumes, therefore, that most of Lamb's readers had never read the play, nor were they likely to read it soon thereafter.

26. Lamb, 31 (his italics).

27. Ibid., 40.

28. Sir Walter Scott, ed. [?], *The Ancient British Drama,* 3 vols. (London: Miller, 1810).

29. Ibid., v–vi.

30. David Erskine Baker, ed., *Biographia Dramatica* (London: Longman, Hurst, Rees, Orme and Brown, 1812).

31. J. P. Collier, from the *Edinburgh Review* 1 (August 1982): 151–52.

32. See Jerome McGann's discussion of Coleridge and Hegel in chap. 4 of *The Romantic Ideology: A Critical Investigation* (Chicago: University of Chicago Press, 1983).

33. C. W. Dilke, ed., *Old English Plays* (London: Whittingham and Rowland, 1814, reprint, 1816).

34. Henry Maitland, in *Blackwood's Magazine*, July and October 1817, 260, 266.

35. See *Specimens of the Table Talk* (16 February 1833), in *The Complete Works of Samuel Taylor Coleridge* (New York: Harper and Brothers, 1871), 6:421–23.

36. J. P. Collier, ed., *A Select Collection of Old Plays*, 3d ed. (London: Septimus Prowett, 1825–27).

37. William Oxberry, ed., *The New English Drama* (London: Simpkin and Marshall, 1818–25). The collection, released from 1818 to 1824, reached 22 volumes, which contained 113 plays.

38. Michael R. Booth et al., *The Revels History of Drama in English* (London: Methuen and Co., 1975), 6:3–5, 7.

39. In 1811, during a production of *Blue Beard*, horses were even introduced on the stage.

40. See G. M. Trevelyan, *A Shortened History of England* (New York: Longmans, Green, and Co., 1942), 453.

41. In his *Specimens*, Lamb also suggests that a new social attitude toward Jews had taken root by saying, as quoted earlier, that the "idea" of the Jew "has nothing in it now revolting." Lamb continues by making the following arcane statement:

> We have tamed the claws of the beast, and pared its nails, and now we take it to our arms, fondle it, write plays to flatter it [see Cumberland]: it is visited by princes, affects a taste, patronises the arts, and is the only liberal and gentleman-like thing in Christendom (31).

One suspects sarcasm in this digression.

42. Richard Cumberland, *The Jew* (London: 1794).

43. Butler, 161.

44. *Blackwood's Magazine*, May 1818, 333, 209–10.

45. Another reviewer in the *European Magazine and London Review* further problematizes the implication of the play's reception. He finds the alterations of Kean's production "too inconsiderable to be noticed." He notes that the tragedy is "generally known" and that it was "much adapted to our stage." (It seems also that there were some problems with the fact that it was performed during the Passover.) (*Blackwood's Magazine*, May 1818, lxxxii, 429–30.)

46. William Oxberry, *Oxberry's Dramatic and Histrionic Anecdotes*, 3 vols. (London: G. Virtue, 1825), 14–15. The anecdote recalls the details of a drunken jaunt that Kean and Oxberry went on.

47. Hazlitt, *Complete Works*, vol. 6.

48. Ibid., 176

49. David Bromwich, *Hazlitt: The Mind of a Critic* (New York and Oxford: Oxford University Press, 1983), 7.

50. Hazlitt, 175.

51. Butler, 172–73.

52. Hazlitt, 175, 177.

53. Bromwich, 6.

54. Hazlitt, 179.

55. Ibid, 203.

56. Ibid., 203.

57. Ibid., 202.

58. Christopher Marlowe, *The Works of Christopher Marlowe*, 3 vols., ed. G. Robinson (London: William Pickering, 1826).
59. Ibid., i–ii.
60. Ibid., iii.
61. Ibid.

Chapter 2. The Foundation of Marlowe Scholarship

1. Christopher Marlowe, *Christopher Marlowe: The Complete Plays*, ed. J. B. Steane (England: Hazlell, Watson, and Viney, 1969), 9, 15.
2. *Monthly Review* 89 (August 1819): 362.
3. *Monthly Review* 93 (September 1820): 61. The reviewer says later that

> Ben Jonson and Drayton have mentioned Marlowe, but not in the manner that implies personal acquaintance; and, as the conduct of Marlowe had not the purest reputation, those in the secret might well be disposed to affect a belief in his personal reality, in order that the errors of Shakespeare's youth might be associated only with the name under which they were perhaps incurred. (63)

4. James Broughton, "Of the Dramatic Writers Who Preceded Shakespeare, and Especially of Christopher Marlowe," *The Gentleman's Magazine*, January–June 1830, c, 3–6, 121–26, 222–24, 313–15, 593–97.
5. *Works*, ed. Robinson, iii.
6. Broughton, "Marlowe," *GM*, (January 1830), 4.
7. Ibid.
8. Francis Meres, *Palladis Tamia: Wit's treasury* (London: P. Short, 1598).
9. See Richard Altick, *The Scholar Adventurers* (New York: The Free Press, 1950), 124–34. Altick observes that the origins of Meres's statement did not come "from any circumstantial fact but from Meres' need of a completing term in his rhetorical equation"; that is, Meres was "drawing a neat euphuistic parallel between classical legend and contemporary fact" (133). The rumor that Marlowe was killed by a rival lover, it seems, originated as the result of a rhetorical conceit in which Meres attempted to compare the death of Lycophron, whom Ovid said was killed by a rival lover, with Marlowe (see Meres's text in Scholars' Facsimiles and Reprints [New York, 1938], 286v and 287r). Wood was basically repeating a 1675 report by Edward Phillips who said that Marlowe "rose from an actor to be a maker of plays" (*Theatrum Poetarum Anglicanorum*, 113). The source of this rumor is unknown.
10. Broughton, "Marlowe," *GM*, January 1830), 4. Broughton was referring to the 1812 edition of the "Biographia Dramatica" edited by Stephen Jones. The "Ben Jonson" rumor was recorded in manuscript by the great gossip John Aubrey (*Brief Lives* [reprint; Ann Arbor: University of Michigan Press, 1957], 178).
11. See Altick, *Scholar Adventurers*, 129.
12. See Leslie Hotson, *Death of Christopher Marlowe* (London: Nonesuch Press; reprint, Cambridge: Harvard University Press, 1925), 17–25.
13. Benet College is now Corpus Christi, and it has been established that Marlowe attended school there on the basis of evidence that has since been uncovered. The various spellings of Marlowe's name in the Cambridge records threw off early scholars. However, Broughton and later Dyce (who first speculated that Marlowe received a Parker scholarship) were on the right track, and they pioneered future discoveries.
14. Broughton, "Marlowe," *GM*, (Feb. 1830) 125.
15. Ibid., (Feb. 1830) 123.

16. Feb., (Feb. 1830) 125.

17. George Charles Smith, *The Ground of the Theatre* (London: Wakefield, 1828).

18. J. L. and Barbara Hammond, *The Age of the Chartists* (London: Longmans, Green and Co., 1930; New York: Augustus M. Kelley, 1967), 255–58.

19. Broughton, "Marlowe," *GM*, (Jan. 1830), 5.

20. Ibid., (Feb. 1830) 122.

21. Ibid., (Feb. 1830) 123.

22 John Payne Collier, *The History of English Dramatic Poetry to the Time of Shakespeare: and Annals of the Stage to the Restoration* (London: John Murray, 1831).

23. See Dewey Ganzel, *Fortune and Men's Eyes: The Career of John Payne Collier* (Oxford: Oxford University Press, 1987), 36.

24. It may be of some interest to the reader that there seems to be a discrepancy between Ganzel and Altick on this point. In *The Scholar Adventurers*, Altick states that *The History of English Dramatic Poetry* gained Collier "entree" to Devonshire's library and to the Bridgewater House library of the Earl of Ellesmere. Ganzel, however, contends that Collier gained access to Devonshire's collection early in 1830, over a year before his history was published. (See also Samuel Schoenbaum, *Shakespeare's Lives* (Oxford: Clarendon Press; New York: Oxford University Press, 1970), 336–37.) Altick and Ganzel also disagree on the matter of Edmond Malone's professional reliability. When referring to the alteration (and even mutilation) of certain Alleyn and Henslowe papers, Altick states that "no suspicion [was] attached to Malone" (151). Ganzel, however, states that Malone treated certain of the Dulwich manuscripts "as his own . . . on occasion cutting autographs from their pages to embellish his books" (46). It is uncertain, however, if Altick and Ganzel are referring to the same mutilations.

25. Collier, *History*, 3:107–12. T. S. Eliot credits the finding of the Spenser borrowings to J. M. Robertson, whose work came years after Collier. Because of the popularity of Eliot's essays, it should be noted that the debt Marlowe owed to Spenser in *Tamburlaine* was recorded by Collier roughly ninety years before Eliot's observations on Marlowe (see Eliot's *Essays on Elizabethan Drama* [New York: Harcourt, Brace and World, 1960], 58–59, and Collier's *History*, 3:117–18). This connection has been "found" several times during the twentieth century.

26. See Altick, *The Scholar Adventurers*, 144–60, and Schoenbaum, 332–61.

27. Some of these were in fact obscene (see Altick, *The Scholar Adventurers*, 152–53).

28. Quoted from the 1826 Pickering preface, xx (ed. Robinson).

29. Ibid., xxiii.

30. Ibid.

31. Ibid.

31. Collier, *History*, 3:113.

32. Ibid., 115–16.

33. *Edinburgh Review*, August 1820, vii, 151–52. Later, in the *History*, Collier elaborates on this matter. Before discussing *Faustus*, which Collier held was Marlowe's second play, he states that

> it may be proper to remark, that I shall follow it [*Faustus*] up by a similar criticism upon his other plays, (as nearly as I can judge in the order in which they were written), with a view to trace the gradual improvement of his [Marlowe's] style and versification. . . . (3:127)

34. Quoted from John Bakeless, *The Tragicall History of Christopher Marlowe*, 2 vols. (reprint, Westport, Conn.: Greenwood Press, 1942), 1:93. See also Schoenbaum, 344.

35. John Payne Collier, *The Poet's Pilgrimage: An Allegorical Poem in Four Cantos* (London: S. Prowett, 1825).

36. Collier, *History*, 3:118.

37. Ibid., 119.

38. Quoted from Bakeless, 2:285.

39. Ibid., 2:285.

40. See Schoenbaum, 348–61, and Bakeless, 196. As late as 1982, Collier's latest biographer credits Collier with establishing Marlowe as the author of *Tamburlaine* although the forgery had been exposed for over one hundred years. And, although the authorship of *Tamburlaine* has since been proven on the strength of other evidence, some of which Collier also recorded, this same biographer cites the forged Henslowe entry as an example of Collier's editorial prowess (Ganzel, 46–47).

41. Samuel A. Tannenbaum, "Study of the Collier Leaf," in *Shakesperian Scraps and Other Elizabethan Fragments* (New York: Columbia University Press, 1933), 178.

42. A. D. Wraight, *In Search of Christopher Marlowe: A Pictoral Biography* (London: Macdonald, 1965), 224–32.

43. *Index of English Literary Manuscripts*, compiled by Peter Beal. vol. 1, pt. 2 (Mansell, London: R. R. Bowker Co., 1980), 325. See also J. Q. Adams, "The Massacre at Paris Leaf," *The Library* 14, 4th ser. (1934): 447–69, and J. M. Nosworthy, "The Marlowe Manuscript," *The Library* 26, 4th ser. (1946): 158–71. During a Marlowe Society meeting at the 1989 MLA Convention, Professor Laurie Maguire presented paleographical evidence that indicated that the leaf is not in Marlowe's hand.

44. Collier, *History*, 133–34.

45. Ganzel, 96.

46. Ibid., 50.

47. Alexander Dyce, *Remarks on J. P. Collier's and Mr. C. Knight's Editions of Shakespeare* (London, 1844), Preface.

48. *The Works of Christopher Marlowe*, ed. Alexander Dyce, 2d ed., 3 vols. (London: William Pickering, 1850).

49. Ibid., xvii.

50. Dyce, though, deserves the credit for this highly important discovery.

51. Marlowe's *Works*, ed. Dyce, x.

52. Ibid., i.

53. Ibid., iv.

54. Ibid., xxv.

55. Richard Schrader, "Alexander Dyce," in *The Reminiscences of Alexander Dyce* (Columbus: Ohio State University Press), 4–6.

56. Marlowe's *Works*, ed. Dyce, vi.

57. Ibid., xv.

58. Ibid., xx–xxi.

59. Ibid., xi–xii.

60. Ibid., xxiv.

61. Ibid., xxv.

62. Ibid.

63. *The Works of Christopher Marlowe*, ed. Francis Cunningham (London: Albert J. Crocker Brothers, 1870), x.

64. *The Works of Christopher Marlowe*, ed. A. H. Bullen (London: Nimmo; Boston: Houghton Mifflin, 1885).

Chapter 3. The Institutionalization of Marlowe

1. For examples and further references, see Millar Maclure, *Marlowe: The Critical Heritage* (London: Routledge and Kegan Paul, 1979), and Kenneth Friedenreich *Christopher Marlowe: An Annotated Bibliography of Criticism since 1850* (London: Scarecrow Press, 1979). Friedenreich's introduction provides an engaging examination of how Darwinistic theories of evolution shaped the perceptions of literary historians during the late nineteenth century.

2. *Works*, ed. Bullen, preface.

3. John Gross, *The Rise and Fall of the Man of Letters* (London: Weidenfeld and Nicolson, 1969), 178.

4. See Chris Baldick, *The Social Mission of English Criticism: 1848–1932* (Oxford: Clarendon Press, 1983),chap. 2, for an analysis of Arnold's ideology, and chap. 3 for a discussion of how and why nineteenth-century educators came to see English as a "civilizing" subject. For a further treatment of the institutionalization of English studies during the late nineteenth century and how it affects modern criticism, see Gerald Graff, *Professing Literature: An Institutional History* (Chicago: University of Chicago Press, 1987). Terry Eagleton's *Literary Theory* (Minneapolis: University of Minnesota Press, 1983) also provides a brief overview of the social and political forces that influenced the rise of English (18–30). Both Gross and Altick (see following note) provide valuable discussion of this phenomenon as well.

5. See Richard Altick, *The English Common Reader: A Social History of the Mass Reading Public, 1800–1900*, (Chicago: The University of Chicago Press, 1975), 277–83.

6. Robert Chambers, ed., *Cyclopaedia of English Literature*, 2 vols. (London: W. and R. Chambers, 1843–44). The *Cyclopaedia* made Altick's nineteenth-century "Best Seller List" (ibid.).

7. Dionysius Lardner, ed., *The Cabinet Cyclopaedia* (London: Rees, Orme, Brown, and Green, 1831–51), and Henry Hallam, ed., *Introduction to the Literature of Europe in the Fifteenth, Sixteenth, and Seventeenth Centuries* (Paris: Baudry's European Library, 1839). Lardner's edition covered the lives of both literary and scientific men, while Hallam's reviewed the history of English and Continental literature.

8. Quoted from *Cyclopaedia of English Literature*, ed. Robert Chambers, 2 vols. (Boston: Gould, Kendall and Lincoln, 1847), 1:173, col. 2.

9. Ibid., 171, col. 2.

10. Ibid.

11. Gross, 193.

12. William Spalding, *The History of English Literature*, 3d ed. (Edinburgh: Oliver and Boyd, 1855).

13. Ibid., 256.

14. Gross, 193–94.

15. Thomas Shaw, *A Complete Manual of English Literature* (New York: Sheldon and Co., 1867).

16. Ibid., 126.

17. Henry Morley, *A First Sketch of English Literature* (London, Paris, and New York: Cassell, Petter, and Galpin, 1873).

18. Ibid., 417–18.

19. Tucker Brooke, in a literary history provided for students in 1948, bowdlerizes Marlowe's biography in much the same way as his nineteenth-century predecessors. After providing evidence of Marlowe's "high" personal character, Brooke treats the matter of his death in an abrupt manner.

"Slain by a bawdy serving man, a rival of his in his lewd love," Meres wrote of Marlowe in this same year [as Blount's dedication to *Hero and Leander*] 1598, basing his statement upon that of a Puritan pamphleteer, Thomas Beard, who based his on hearsay. Factually, the charge has been disproved by Mr. Hotson's discovery of the death record; more fundamentally, it is disproved by *Hero and Leander*. (*A Literary History of England*, ed. Albert C. Baugh [New York: Appleton-Century-Crofts, 1948], 514)

Brooke goes on to suggest that the purity of Marlowe's poetic fragment reflects Marlowe's own moral purity. What Brooke fails to mention is that, while Hotson did discredit Meres, the documents he discovered indicated that Marlowe was slain during a tavern brawl in self-defense by a man named Ingram Friser. In the light of other discoveries concerning the people who were present at Marlowe's death, critics have come to suspect conspiracy or foul play on the part of the authorities. However, Hotson's research in no way provides supporting evidence for Marlowe's moral purity as Brooke indicates above.

20. Spalding, 256, and Shaw, 126.

21. *Works*, ed. Bullen, xxxviii.

22. Interestingly enough, this high evaluation has survived. Irving Ribner, in his 1966 edition of the play (New York: Odyssey Press), calls it both "the greatest achievement of Christopher Marlowe" and "the finest example of English tragedy up to its time" (vi). It is also the one Marlovian drama selected by the current *Norton Anthology of English Literature*.

23. John Anster, translator of *Goethe's Faust*, to which is prefixed Marlowe's *Faustus*, ed. with an intro. by Henry Morley (London, 1883), and Hermann Breymann, *Faustus*, (Heilbronn: Henninger, 1883), which has the 1604 and 1616 texts on opposite pages.

24. See Otto Heller, *Faust and Faustus: A Study of Goethe's Relation to Marlowe* (St. Louis: Washington University Press, 1931), 9–11, on the neglect of the matter of Marlowe's influence on Goethe during the late nineteenth and early twentieth centuries.

25. G. H. Lewes, *The Life of Goethe*, 2d ed. (London: George Routledge and Sons; New York: E. P. Dutton, 1864), 319.

26. Shaw's *Manual* was a follow-up to his *Outlines of English Literature* (Philadelphia: Blanchard and Lea, 1859). The *Outlines*, according to Shaw, had "no pretensions whatsoever to the title of a complete Course of English Literature" (v), whereas the *Manual* was "a complete History of English Literature" which had "a special view to the requirements of Students" (3). It is interesting to note that the details of Wood's account of Marlowe's lewd and blasphemous death as included in the *Outlines*, whereas they are omitted from the *Manual*.

27. Edward Dowden, *Transcripts and Studies* (London: Kegan Paul, Trench and Co., 1888), 433.

28. For an understanding of how German romanticism was reproduced as an English literary theory, see Jerome J. McCann, *The Romantic Ideology: A Critical Investigation* (Chicago: University of Chicago Press, 1983), chap. 4, on the changes of the romantic ideology from Hegel to Coleridge.

29. See Kathryn Ludwigson, *Edward Dowden* (New York: Twayne Publishers, 1973), 15.

30. Ibid., 76.

31. Edward Dowden, *Shakespeare: A Critical Study of His Mind and Art* (London: Kegan, Paul, Trench, Trubner, 1892), 35.

32. Ibid., 1–2.

33. Ibid., 9.
34. Ibid., 25.
35. Dowden, *Transcripts and Studies*, 99, 100.
36. Ibid., 435.
37. Ibid., 436.
38. Ibid., 102.
39. Ibid., 438.
40. Hippolyte Taine, *A History of English Literature*, trans. H. Van Laun (Edinburgh: Edmonston and Douglas, 1873).
41. Ibid., 385.
42. Ibid., 386. Taine's presumptiveness, however, is in line with what many twentieth-century critics have concluded were Marlowe's actual statements. However, Taine's commentary precedes a bulk of research that provides more substantial proof of Marlowe's associations with free thinkers and his possible atheism. In 1946, Paul Kocher in *Christopher Marlowe: A Study of his Thought, Learning, and Character* (Chapel Hill: University of North Carolina Press, 1946) provides an in-depth study of what he found to be the apparent theological structure of the note. He argues that "Baines seems to be taking notes either direct from a manuscript written by Marlowe or from some lecture which he delivered" (33). Kocher's discussion is erudite and well reasoned, but it rests almost completely on the notion that the note has a unified structure and is therefore Marlovian in origin (Kocher's numerology has been provided in Appendix B). Even with the advantage of additional research, the exact connection between Marlowe and Baines is still uncertain.
43. Taine, 386. See also my Appendix A.
44. A descendant version of the argument between the romantic idealist and the historical realist can be viewed in Roy Battenhouse's *Marlowe's "Tamburlaine"* (Nashville: Vanderbilt University Press, 1941). At the beginning of his discussion, Battenhouse pits himself against "romantics," such as Boas, Ingram, and Ellis-Fermor, who see Marlowe as unorthodox. He goes on to expose how, in his view, the play was "determined" by the precepts of Renaissance moral philosophy. Unlike Taine, however, Battenhouse defends the playwright.
45. William Minto, *Characteristics of English Poets from Chaucer to Shirley* (Edinburgh and London: William Blackwood, 1874).
46. Ibid., vi.
47. Ibid., 302.
48. A. W. Ward, *A History of English Dramatic Literature to the Death of Queen Anne* 2d ed. (London: MacMillan and Co., 1899), 363.
49. This has occurred as late as the 1950s. For instance, in *The Overreacher* (Cambridge: Harvard University Press, 1952), Harry Levin, speaking of the satisfaction moralists gained from the accounts of Marlowe's death, says that "[f]or Marlowe to have been killed in a tavern brawl which he provoked—to have been stabbed at Deptford, as it turned out, by his own dagger—was to have been outdone at his own game by the very hand of Providence. *It was, with a vengeance, the Atheist's tragedy*" (4) [my italics]. Perhaps Levin was referring to *The Atheist's Tragedy* (1611) by Tourneur. A title is not indicated, however, and the reference to an "Atheist's tragedy" at the end of a biographical description of Marlowe in 1952 is startling.
50. T. H. Ward, *The English Poets* (London: MacMillan and Co., 1880), 411.
51. *Works*, ed. Bullen, xiv.
52. Ward, *The English Poets*, 411–12.
53. Ibid., 414.
54. Ibid., 417.

Chapter 4. Marlowe among the Aesthetes

1. Philip Horton, *Hart Crane: The Life of an American Poet* (New York: Octagon Books, 1937, reprint, 1976), 145, 311.

2. Richard Hengist (Henry) Horne, "The Death of Christopher Marlowe," *The Monthly Repository* 12, no. 1 (July–August 1837): 128–40. Also R. H. Horne, *The Death of Christopher Marlowe: A Tragedy in One Act* (London: Saunders and Otley, 1837).

3. Horne, "Death of Marlowe," 128–29.

4. Ibid., 130.

5. Ibid., 131–32.

6. Thomas Beard, *The Theatre of God's Judgement* (London: Islip and Spark, 1631), lib. I, chap. 25.

7. Horne, "Death of Marlowe," 138.

8. Ibid., 134.

9. Ibid., 133. The term "spirits of the age" seems allusive in the light of Hazlitt's *The Spirit of the Age*, and it anticipates Horne's own *New Spirit of the Ages*.

10. Ibid., 365.

11. Horne, *The Death of Christopher Marlowe*, dedication.

12. Leigh Hunt, *Imagination and Fancy* (London: Smith, Elder, and Co., 1844), 1.

13. Ibid., 138.

14. Ibid., 139.

15. Ibid., 141. See also 141–43. Hunt quotes Barabas's opening speech (1.1.1–48) and italicizes certain lines in order to demonstrate their "wonderful sweetness." For example, the line *"Fie, what a trouble 'tis to count this trash"* is marked for this purpose.

16. Thus the notion of Marlowe as a radical had an inauspicious but early origin. It has not been until recently that the radical characteristics of Marlowe's life and works have been discussed with any force. Most notably, Stephen Greenblatt, in *Renaissance Self-Fashioning* (Chicago and London: The University of Chicago Press, 1980), and Jonathan Dollimore, in *Radical Tragedy* (Great Britain: The Harvester Press, 1984), have suggested that Marlowe's plays demonstrate a a willful subversiveness. This is a strained comparison, however, because the radical Marlowe of the 1980s bears little resemblance to the rebellious Marlowe of the 1830 and '40s.

17. Dowden, *Transcripts and Studies*, 437.

18. A. C. Swinburne, *George Chapman: A Critical Essay* (London: Chatto and Windus, 1875), 164.

19. For a thorough analysis of the principles of Swinburne's criticism, see Robert L. Peters, *The Crowns of Apollo* (Detroit: Wayne State University Press, 1965), chap. 2.

20. G. B. Shaw, *Dramatic Opinions and Essays* (reprint, New York: Brentano's, 1925), 37.

21. *The Complete Works of Algernon Charles Swinburne*, vol. 5, ed. Edmund Gosse and Thomas Wise (London: William Heinemann; reprint, New York: Gabriel Wells, 1925), 171.

22. Swinburne, *Chapman*, 152–53.

23. Quoted from Fredson Bowers, *The Complete Works of Christopher Marlowe* (Cambridge: Cambridge University Press, 1973), 2: 453–54.

24. Swinburne, *Chapman*, 165.

25. Quoted from A. H. Bullen, ed., *The Tragical History of Doctor Faustus*, as revived by the Elizabethan Stage Society under the direction of William Poel, (London, 1904), prologue.

26. Swinburne, *Chapman*, 166.

27. See Phyllis Grosskurth, *John Addington Symonds: A Biography* (London: Longmans, Green and Co., 1964), 272–75.

28. Grosskurth, 122, 155, 233.

29. J. A. Symonds, *Shakspeare's Predecessors in the English Drama* (London: Smith, Elder, & Co., 1884), 586.

30. Ibid., 606.

31. Ibid., 666.

32. Ibid., 668.

33. Churton Collins, Review of *Shakspeare's Predecessors*, *The Quarterly Review* 161 (July–October 1885): 330–81.

34. Symonds, *Shakspeare's Predecessors*, 608.

35. Ibid.

36. Ibid., 609.

37. Ibid., 668.

38. Most notably Havelock Ellis, *Studies in the Psychology of Sex* (Philadelphia: F. A. Davis Co., 1919).

39. See, specifically, Vincent Brome, *Havelock Ellis: Philosopher of Sex* (London: Boston, and Henley: Routledge and Kegan Paul, 1979), and Houston Peterson, *Havelock Ellis: Philosopher of Love* (Boston and New York: Houghton Mifflin Co., 1928).

40. Havelock Ellis and J. A. Symonds, *Sexual Inversion* (London: Wilson and Macmillan, 1897; reprint, New York: Arno Press, 1975), 123.

41. Vizetelly's printings of Zola, in fact, later won him a term in jail.

42. Havelock Ellis, *My Life* (Boston: Houghton Mifflin Co., 1939), 208.

43. Havelock Ellis, ed., *Christopher Marlowe* (London: Vizetelly, 1887).

44. Ellis clearly forwards this thesis in *The New Spirit* (Boston: Houghton Mifflin, London: G. Bell, 1890).

45. Ellis, ed., *Christopher Marlowe*, xxx.

46. Ibid., xviii.

47. Ritson, however, published an uncensored version of the note in 1782 (see chap. 1, n. 14, and Appendix B herein).

48. See Peterson, 177.

49. Ellis, *My Life*, 209.

50. For the details of how Symonds's death related to the publication of *Sexual Inversion*, see Grosskurth, 284–94.

51. Ellis and Symonds, *Sexual Inversion*, 15, 18. In a recent study entitled *Marlowe and the Politics of Elizabethan Theatre* (New York: St. Martin's Press, 1986), Simon Sheperd lampoons two seemingly homophobic responses to Marlowe's sexuality during the twentieth century, thus demonstrating that the controversy begun by Ellis and Symonds is still continuing even a century later (xii). In all fairness, however, the view of Marlowe as homosexual, carrying with it the implication that he can be compared personally or sociologically with current-day gays, was invented by Ellis and Symonds.

52. See Schoenbaum's discussion of Marlowe as seducer in Oscar Wilde's *Portrait of Mr. W. H.* (448) and also his review of various "rivals" (458–59).

53. Most of these were for the most part inconsequential. See J. G. Lewis's pamphlet *Christopher Marlowe: Outlines of His Life and Works. A lecture written by J. G. Lewis of the Inland Revenue and delivered at Canterbury on the 8th May 1890, in aid of the Marlowe Memorial Fund by Ralph Stewart, Elocutionist.*

For further dramatic treatments of Marlowe, see W. L. Courtney's play, "Kit Marlowe's Death." in *Universal Review* 6: 356–71, reprinted in *Studies at Leisure*

(1892), also produced by Arthur Bourchier, with Cyril Maud at Shaftesbury Theatre, 4 July 1890, and revived at the St. James Theatre in 1892. There is in the British Museum James Hosken's *Christopher Marlowe, a tragedy*, which was published in 1896. Also, Josephine Peabody wrote a play in 1901 entitled *Marlowe, a drama in five acts*, which was produced in 1905 at Radcliffe College in Cambridge, Mass. Poems "To Marlowe" were written by Ernest Rhys, John Le Gay, and Brereton Arthur Bayldon in 1894, 1896, and 1899, respectively.

Conclusion

1. Maclure, 23.
2. Friedenreich, 1, 4–5.
3. Ibid., 12, 13.
4. Levin, 8.
5. Greenblatt, 220–21.
6. Gary Taylor, *Reinventing Shakespeare* (New York: Weidenfeld and Nicolson, 1989).

Works Cited

Altick, Richard D. *The English Common Reader: A Social History of the Mass Reading Public, 1800–1900*. Chicago: The University of Chicago Press, 1957.

———. *The Scholar Adventurers*. New York: The Free Press, 1950.

Aubrey, John. *Brief Lives*. Reprint. Ann Arbor: University of Michigan Press, 1957.

Bakeless, John. *The Tragicall History of Christopher Marlowe*. 2 vols. Reprint. Westport, Conn.: Greenwood Press, 1942.

Baker, David Erskine, ed. *Biographia Dramatica*. Originally compiled to the year 1764 by Baker; continued to 1782 by Isaac Reed; brought to November 1811 by Stephen Jones. London: Longman, Hurst, Rees, Orme, and Brown, 1812.

Baldick, Chris. *The Social Mission of English Criticism: 1848–1932*. Oxford: Clarendon Press, 1983.

Battenhouse, Roy W. *Marlowe's "Tamburlaine": A Study in Renaissance Moral Philosophy*. Nashville: Vanderbilt University Press, 1941.

Beard, Thomas. *The Theatre of God's Judgement*. London: Islip and Spark, 1631.

Boas, F. S. *Marlowe and His Circle*. 1929. Reprint. New York: Russell & Russell, 1969.

Booth, Michael R., et al. *The Revels History of Drama in English*. Vol. 6. London: Methuen and Co., 1975.

Bove, Paul. *Intellectuals in Power: A Genealogy of Critical Humanism*. New York: Columbia University Press, 1986.

Bowers, Fredson, ed. *The Complete Works of Christopher Marlowe*. Cambridge: Cambridge University Press, 1973.

Bromwich, David. *Hazlitt: The Mind of a Critic*. New York and Oxford: Oxford University Press, 1983.

Brome, Vincent. *Havelock Ellis; Philosopher of Sex*. London, Boston, and Henley: Routledge & Kegan Paul, 1979.

Brooke, Tucker. "The Reputation of Christopher Marlowe." *Transactions of the Connecticut Academy of Arts and Sciences* 25 (June 1922): 347–408.

———. "Christopher Marlowe." In *A Literary History of England*, edited by Albert C. Baugh, 508–18. New York: Appleton-Century-Crofts, Inc., 1948.

Broughton, James. "Of the Dramatic Writers Who Preceded Shakespeare, and Especially of Christopher Marlowe." *The Gentleman's Magazine*, January–June 1830, c, 3–6, 121–26, 222–24, 313–15, 593–97.

Brydges, Sir Egerton. *Restituta*. London: Longmans et al., 1814–16.

Bullen, A. H., ed. *The Tragical History of Doctor Faustus*, as revised by the Elizabethan Stage Society under the direction of William Poel. London, 1904.

———, ed. *The Works of Christopher Marlowe*. London: Nimmo; Boston: Houghton Mifflin, 1885.

Butler, Marilyn. *Romantics, Rebels, and Reactionaries: English Literature and its Back-ground 1760–1830*. Oxford: Oxford University Press, 1982.

Carlyle, Thomas. *The French Revolution*. New York: Random House, 1934.

Chambers, Robert, ed. *Cyclopaedia of English Literature*. 2 vols. London: W. and R. Chambers, 1843–44.

———, ed. *Cyclopaedia of English Literature*. 2 vols. Boston: Gould, Kendall, and Lincoln, 1847.

Chapple, C. *Old English Poets*. London: Chapple, 1820.

Cibber, Theophilus. *The Lives of the Poets of Great Britain and Ireland to the Time of Dean Swift*. London: R. Griffiths, 1753. (Vol. 1 entry on Marlowe probably by Robert Shiels.)

Coleridge, Samuel Taylor. *Specimens of the Table Talk*. In *The Complete Works of Samuel Taylor Coleridge*. New York: Harper and Brothers, 1871.

Collier, J. P. From the *Edinburgh Review*, June 1820; vi, 521; August 1820; vii, 151–52.

———. *The History of English Dramatic Poetry to the Time of Shakespeare: and Annals of the Stage to the Restoration*. 3 vols. London: John Murray, 1831.

———. *The Poet's Pilgrimage: an Allegorical Poem in Four Cantos*. London: S. Prowett, 1825.

———, ed. *A Select Collection of Old Plays*. 3d ed. London: Septimus Prowett, 1825–27.

Collins, Churton. "Shakespeare's Predessors in the English Drama." *The Quarterly Review* 161 (July–October 1885): 330–81.

Cumberland, Richard. *The Jew*. London, 1794.

Cunningham, Francis, ed. *The Works of Christopher Marlowe*. London: Albert J. Crocker Brothers, 1885.

Dilke, C. W., ed. *Old English Plays*. London: Whittingham and Rowland, 1814.

———. *Old plays: being a continuation of Dodsley's collection*. London: Rodwell and Martin, 1816.

Dodsley, Robert, ed. *A Select Collection of Old Plays*. 1st ed. 12 vols. London, 1744. (Vol. 1 contains the preface; *Edward II* is in vol. 2.)

———, ed. *A Select Collection of Old Plays*. 2d ed. Edited by Isaac Reed. London: J. Nichols for J. Dodsley, 1780.

———, ed. *A Select Collection of Old Plays*. 3d ed. Edited by J. P. Collier. London: Septimus Prowett, 1825–27.

Dollimore, Jonathan. *Radical Tragedy: Religion, Ideology and Power in the Drama of Shakespeare and his Contemporaries*. Great Britain: The Harvester Press, 1984.

Dowden, Edward. *Shakespeare: A Critical Study of His Mind and Art*. London: Kegan Paul, Trench, Trubner, 1892.

———. *Transcripts and Studies*. London: Kegan Paul, Trench and Co., 1888.

Dyce, Alexander. *Remarks on Mr. J. P. Collier's and Mr. C. Knight's Editions of Shake-speare*. London, 1844.

———, ed. *The Works of Christopher Marlowe*. London: William Pickering, 1826.

Eagleton, Terry. *Literary Theory: An Introduction*. Minneapolis: University of Min-nesota Press, 1983.

Eliot, T. S. *Essays on Elizabethan Drama*. New York: Harcourt, Brace and World, 1960.

Ellis, Havelock. *My Life: Autobiography of Havelock Ellis*. Boston: Houghton Mifflin Co., 1939.

———. *The New Spirit*. Boston: Houghton-Mifflin; London: G. Bell, 1890.

———. *Studies in the Psychology of Sex*. Philadelphia: F. A. Davis Co., 1919.

———, ed. *Christopher Marlowe*. London: Vizetelly, 1887.

Ellis, Havelock, and J. A. Symonds. *Sexual Inversion*. London: Wilson and Macmillan, 1897; New York: Arno Press, 1975.

Foucault, Michel. "What Is an Author?" Translated by Josue V. Harari. In *Textual Strategies: Perspectives in Post-Structuralist Criticism*, edited by Josue V. Harari, 141–60. Ithaca: Cornell University Press, 1979.

Friedenreich, Kenneth. *Christopher Marlowe: An Annotated Bibliography of Criticism since 1950*. London: Scarecrow Press, 1979.

Ganzel, Dewey. *Fortune and Men's Eyes: The Career of John Payne Collier*. Oxford: Oxford University Press, 1982.

Graff, Gerald. *Professing Literature: An Institutional History*. Chicago: University of Chicago Press, 1987.

Greenblatt, Stephen. *Renaissance Self-Fashioning*. Chicago and London: University of Chicago Press, 1980.

Greene, Robert. "A Groats-worth of Wit; Bought with a Million of Repentance." Edited by Sir Egerton Brydges. Printed at the Private Press of Lee Priory by Johnson and Warwick, 1813.

Gross, John. *The Rise and Fall of the Man of Letters*. London: Weidenfeld and Nicolson, 1969.

Grosskurth, Phyllis. *John Addington Symonds: A Biography*. London: Longmans, Green and Co., 1964.

Hallam, Henry, ed. *Introduction to the Literature of Europe in the Fifteenth, Sixteenth, and Seventeenth Centuries*. Vol. 2. Paris: Baudry's European Library, 1839.

Hammond, J. L. and Barbara. *The Age of the Chartists, 1832–1852: A Study of Discontent*. London: Longmans, Green & Co., 1930. Reprint. New York: Augustus M. Kelley, 1967.

Hazlitt, William. *The Complete Works of William Hazlitt*. Edited by P. P. Howe. Vol. 6. London: J. M. Dent and Sons, 1931.

Heller, Otto. *Faust and Faustus: A Study of Goethe's Relation to Marlowe*. St. Louis: Washington University Press, 1931.

Horne, Richard Hengist (Henry). "The Death of Christopher Marlowe." *The Monthly Repository* 11, no. 1 (July–December 1837): 128–140.

———. *The Death of Christopher Marlowe: A Tragedy in One Act*. London: Saunders and Otley, 1837.

Horton, Philip. *Hart Crane: The Life of an American Poet*. New York: Octagon Books, 1937. Reprint, 1976.

Hotson, Leslie. *Death of Christopher Marlowe*. London: Nonesuch Press. Reprint. Cambridge: Harvard University Press, 1925.

Hunt, Leigh. *Imagination and Fancy*. London: Smith, Elder, and Co., 1844.

Index of English Literary Manuscripts. Compiled by Peter Beal. Vol. 1, pt. 2. Mansell, London: R. R. Bowker Co., 1980.

Ingleby, C. M. "Spurious ballads, &c., affecting Shakespeare and Marlowe." *Academy* 9 (1 April 1876): 313.

Kocher, Paul. *Christopher Marlowe: A Study of his Thought, Learning, and Character.* Chapel Hill: University of North Carolina Press, 1946.

Lamb, Charles. *Specimens of English Dramatic Poets Who Lived About the Time of Shakespeare.* London: Longman, Hurst, Rees, Orme, 1808.

Langbaine, Gerard. *Account of the English Dramatick Poets.* Oxford, 1691.

Lardner, Dionysius, ed. *The Cabinet Cyclopaedia.* London: Rees, Orme, Brown, and Green, 1831–51.

Levin, Harry. *The Overreacher: A Study of Christopher Marlowe.* Cambridge: Harvard University Press, 1952.

Lewes, G. H. *The Life of Goethe.* 2d ed. London: George Routledge and Sons; New York: E. P. Dutton, 1864.

A Literary History of England. Edited by Albert C. Baugh. New York: Appleton-Century-Crofts, Inc., 1948.

Ludwigson, Kathryn. *Edward Dowden.* New York: Twayne Publishers, 1973.

Maclure, Millar. *Marlowe: The Critical Heritage.* London: Routledge and Kegan Paul, 1979.

Maitland, Henry. In *Blackwood's Magazine,* July 1817, October 1817.

Marlowe, Christopher. *The Works of Christopher Marlowe.* 3 vols. Edited by G. Robinson. London: William Pickering, 1826.

———. *The Works of Christopher Marlowe.* 2d edition. 3 vols. Edited by Alexander Dyce. London: William Pickering, 1850.

———. *The Works of Christopher Marlowe.* Edited by Francis Cunningham. London: Albert J. Crocker Brothers, 1870.

———. *The Works of Christopher Marlowe.* Edited by A. H. Bullen. London: Nimmo; Boston: Houghton Mifflin, 1885.

———. *Christopher Marlowe.* Edited by Havelock Ellis. London: Vizetelly, 1887.

———. *Dr. Faustus.* Edited by Irving Ribner. New York: Odyssey Press, 1966.

———. *Christopher Marlowe: The Complete Plays.* Edited by J. B. Steane. England: Hazell Watson & Viney, 1969.

———. *The Complete Works.* Edited by Fredson Bowers. Cambridge: Cambridge University Press, 1973.

Meres, Francis. *Palladis Tamia: Wit's treasury.* London: P. Short, 1598.

McGann, Jerome J. *The Romantic Ideology: A Critical Investigation.* Chicago: University of Chicago Press, 1983.

Minto, William. *Characteristics of English Poets from Chaucer to Shirley.* Edinburgh and London: William Blackwood, 1874.

Morley, Henry. *First Sketch of English Literature.* London, Paris, and New York: Cassell, Petter, and Galpin, 1873.

Old English Drama. Vol. 2. London: Hurst, Robinson, and Co.; Edinburgh: Constable, 1825.

Oxberry, William, ed. *The New English Drama, with prefatory remarks, biographical sketches, and notes, critical and explanatory; being the only edition existing which is faithfully marked with stage business and stage directions, as performed at the Theatres Royal.* London: Simpkin and Marhsall, 1818–25.

Oxberry's Dramatic Biography and Histrionic Anecdotes. 3 vols. London: G. Virtue, 1825.

Penley, Samson. *The Jew of Malta.* With alterations and additions. London: Text of Kean's 1818 Drury Lane Production, 1813.

Peters, Robert L. *The Crowns of Apollo: A Study in Victorian Criticism and Aesthetics.* Detroit: Wayne State University Press, 1965.

Peterson, Houston. *Havelock Ellis: Philosopher of Love.* Boston and New York: Houghton Mifflin Co., 1928.

Phillips, Edward. *Theatrum Poetarum or a Compleat Collection of the Poets.* London: Charles Smith, 1675.

Poel, William, dir. *The Tragical History of Doctor Faustus.* As revived by the Elizabethan Stage society under the direction of William Poel. Edited by A. H. Bullen. London, 1904.

Reed, Isaac, ed. *A Select Collection of Old Plays.* 2d ed. London: J. Nichols for J. Dodsley, 1780.

Review of Hazlitt's *Lectures on the Literature of the Age of Elizabeth. Monthly Review* 93 (September 1820): 59–67.

Review of *The Jew of Malta. Blackwood's Magazine,* May 1818, iii, 209–10.

Review of *The Jew of Malta. European Magazine, and London Review,* May 1818, lxxiii, 429–30.

Review of Nathan Drake's *Shakespeare and His Times. Monthly Review* 89 (August 1819): 357–71.

Ritson, Joseph. "Observations on the First Three Volumes of the *History of English Poetry,* a Familiar Letter to the Author." London: J. Stockdale, 1782.

Robinson, G., ed. *The Works of Christopher Marlowe.* 3 vols. London: William Pickering, 1826.

Schoenbaum, Samuel. *Shakespeare's Lives.* Oxford: Clarendon Press; New York: Oxford University Press, 1970.

Said, Edward. *Orientalism.* New York: Pantheon Books, 1978.

Scott, Walter ed.(?) *The Ancient British Drama.* 3 vols. London: Miller, 1810.

Schrader, Richard. *The Reminiscences of Alexander Dyce.* Columbus: Ohio State University Press, 1972.

Shaw, G. B. *Dramatic Opinions and Essays.* Reprint. New York: Brentano's, 1925.

Shaw, Thomas. *A Complete Manual of English Literature.* New York: Sheldon and Co., 1867.

———. *Outlines of English Literature.* Philadelphia: Blanchard and Lea, 1859.

Shepherd, Simon. *Marlowe and the Politics of Elizabethan Theatre.* New York: St. Martin's Press, 1986.

Shiels, Robert. Entry on Marlowe in Theophilus Cibber, *The Lives of the Poets of Great Britain and Ireland to the Time of Dean Swift.* London: R. Griffiths, 1753.

Singer, S. W. *Select Early English Poets.* Chiswick: C. Wittingham, 1821.

Smith, George Charles. *The Ground of the Theatre.* London: Wakefield, 1828.

Spalding, William. *The History of English Literature*. 3d ed. Edinburgh: Oliver and Boyd, 1855.

Stephen, Leslie, and Sidney Lee, eds. *The Dictionary of National Biography*. Oxford: Oxford University Press, 1917.

Straus, Ralph. *Robert Dodsley: Poet, Publisher and Playwright*. London: John Lane at the Bodley Head, 1910.

Swinburne, A. C. *George Chapman: A Critical Essay*. London: Chatto and Windus, 1875.

———. *The Complete Works of Algernon Charles Swinburne*. Vol. 5. Edited by Edmund Gosse and Thomas Wise. London: William Heinemann. Reprint. New York: Gabriel Wells, 1925.

Symonds, J. A. "A Problem in Greek Ethics." Privately printed in 1883 and included in Ellis's *Sexual Inversion* (1897).

———. *The Renaissance in Italy*. 7 vols. Smith, Elder & Co., 1875–86.

———. *Shakespeare's Predecessors in the English Drama*. London: Smith, Elder, & Co., 1884.

Taine, H. A. *History of English Literature*. translated by H. Van Laun. Edinburgh: Edmonston and Douglas, 1873.

Tannenbaum, Samuel A. "Study of the Collier Leaf." In *Shakespearian scraps and other Elizabethan fragments*. New York: Columbia University Press, 1933.

Tanner, Thomas. *Bibliotheca Britannico-Hibernica*. 1748. Fac. reprint. Tucson: Aucax Press, 1963.

Taylor, Gary. *Reinventing Shakespeare: A Cultural History from the Restoration to the Present*. New York: Weidenfeld and Nicolson, 1989.

Trevelyan, G. M. *A Shortened History of England*. New York: Longmans, Green & Co., 1942.

Ward, A. W. *A History of English Dramatic Literature to the Death of Queen Anne*. 2d ed. London: MacMillan and Co., 1899.

Ward, T. H. *The English Poets*. London: MacMillan and Co., 1880.

Warton, Thomas. *The History of English Poetry from the Close of the Eleventh to the Commencement of the Eighteenth Century*. Vol. 4. London: Ward, Lock, and co., 1781.

Winstanley, William. *The Lives of the Most Famous English Poets or the Honour of Parnassus*. London: H. Clark, 1687.

Wood, Anthony à. *Athenae Oxonienses*. 3d ed. Edited by Philip Bliss. Vol. 2. Reprint. London: Rivington et al., 1815.

Wraight, A. D. *In Search of Christopher Marlowe: A Pictorial Biography*. London: Macdonald, 1965.

Index